STUDENT AFFAIRS BY THE NUMBERS

Dear Tori,

I am so honored that you would ask me to sign your book. But do you know what's a greater honor? The honor of teaching you and learning from you. Thank you for the gift of getting to watch you grow. I'm so excited to see how you change lives for the better through education.

Faithfully,

Rishi
Sivam

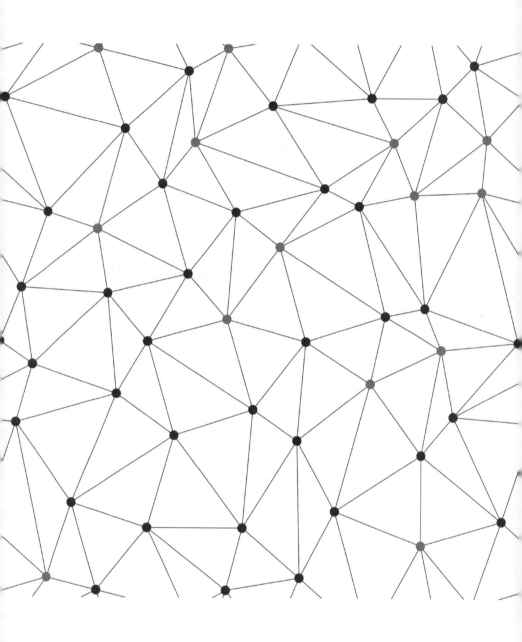

STUDENT AFFAIRS BY THE NUMBERS

Quantitative Research and Statistics for Professionals

Rishi Sriram

STERLING, VIRGINIA

Published by Stylus Publishing, LLC.
22883 Quicksilver Drive
Sterling, Virginia 20166-2102

Library of Congress Cataloging-in-Publication Data
Names: Sriram, Rishi, author.
Title: Student affairs by the numbers: quantitative research and
statistics for professionals/Rishi Sriram.
Description: First edition. |
Sterling, Virginia : Stylus Publishing, 2017. |
Includes bibliographical references and index.
Identifiers: LCCN 2016055484 (print) |
LCCN 2017019965 (ebook) |
ISBN 9781620364536 (uPDF) |
ISBN 9781620364543 (ePub) |
ISBN 9781620364512 (cloth : alk. paper) |
ISBN 9781620364529 (pbk. : alk. paper) |
Subjects: LCSH: Student affairs services--
United States--Evaluation. |
Student affairs services--Research--Statistical methods.
Classification: LCC LB2342.92 (ebook) |
LCC LB2342.92 .S75 2017 (print) |
DDC 371.4--dc23
LC record available at https://lccn.loc.gov/2016055484

13-digit ISBN: 978-1-62036-451-2 (cloth)
13-digit ISBN: 978-1-62036-452-9 (paperback)
13-digit ISBN: 978-1-62036-453-6 (library networkable e-edition)
13-digit ISBN: 978-1-62036-454-3 (consumer e-edition)

Printed in the United States of America

All first editions printed on acid-free paper
that meets the American National Standards Institute
Z39-48 Standard.

Bulk Purchases

Quantity discounts are available for use in workshops and for
staff development.
Call 1-800-232-0223

First Edition, 2017

10   9   8   7   6   5   4   3   2

To Amanda, my Beloved

To Ellis, Lily, and Stella, my darlings

To Jeff Ellis, my mentor

To Francis Shushok, the one who got this all started

To Mom and Dad, for all of your support for all of my dreams

CONTENTS

PREFACE

This book is about using quantitative research and statistics in student affairs work. Statistics is by no means the only way to use your intellect in student affairs, but it is a great tool for doing so. Quantitative research and statistics are becoming increasingly important in student affairs work. Senior administrators, accreditors, government officials, and even parents now have an expectation that higher education institutions will assess and demonstrate program impact. Each year, more research is published on how student affairs work affects students. Understanding this research is a skill in itself, even before attempting to apply research findings in practice. I believe student affairs professionals are educators who help students learn; however, not everyone on a college campus has this same perspective. If those in student affairs are educators, what are they teaching? If learning occurs in students because of the work of student affairs professionals, how does it occur, and to what end? Statistics can help those in student affairs learn more about their own work and its influence on students.

The problem is that not all professionals who work in student affairs have enough knowledge of quantitative research and statistics to incorporate these tools into daily work. Not all who currently work in student affairs have graduate degrees in a field related to higher education. For those who do, many of these programs require at least one course in research methods. These courses are important, but they are rarely enough to form the needed knowledge, attitudes, skills, or behaviors that reflect an acceptable level of research competence. When these graduate students become full-time professionals on college campuses, they enter a practice that may or may not call for them to use whatever competence in quantitative research they gained from graduate school. These new professionals become busy in other activities their work requires. Thereby, learned skills related to statistics can be forgotten and eventually deemed irrelevant.

There are more books on statistics than I care to count or list. When student affairs professionals realize they could use some skill development in this area, they could certainly buy a book currently available and start reading. When I talk to professionals at national conferences, or when I am invited to their campuses to speak, I hear complaints that these books are inaccessible. My graduate students certainly share that opinion. And I agree with them. When I wanted to learn more about statistics, I felt I was learning in spite of books on statistics rather than because of them. Perhaps part of the problem is that books on statistics are written by statisticians. These books often teach more than those in student affairs need to know. They do not differentiate between fundamental knowledge that everyone should grasp and specialized knowledge that is less relevant to a broader audience.

If student affairs professionals are to learn quantitative research and statistics skills, they need a book written for them. You need a book that will meet you where you are and take you by the hand to learn new things that you will find helpful in your work. You need a book that does not share too much knowledge and does not share too little. When I teach these skills at conferences or on campuses, people approach me after my sessions to thank me for meeting them in their current knowledge and stretching them forward in helpful, exciting, and understandable ways. And it is not always student affairs professionals who thank me. I have met several faculty members who did not learn these skills and feel desperate for a way to learn them now.

Every month, esteemed journals related to higher education and student affairs publish the latest research on colleges, college students, and student affairs work. The quantitative methods used are increasingly complex. It is difficult, if not impossible, to apply the findings of these research studies to student affairs practice without understanding the methods and results. But even more important, these studies do not represent the best research out there. The best research is the research rarely published—the small, internal studies done on single campuses to discover, explore, and improve. The best research studies are the ones that answer your questions about your students. Reading a journal article is a great way to learn and can certainly lead to new ideas for your work. However, no research study will take the place of your own research on your own campus.

Ultimately, this book represents what I think every student affairs professional should know about quantitative research and statistics. This is a judgment call on my part. Some will argue that professionals should know more than what is in this book. I am all for professionals knowing more than what is offered here, and in the chapters I recommend some books that can help those who want to take the next step in their knowledge. Others might claim that professionals have done just fine in their work without knowing what is in this book. Perhaps. College students have not done just fine, however. There is a need on college campuses for ways to better promote student retention, engagement, achievement, and learning. Students deserve better, and student affairs professionals are part of the answer.

Overview of Contents

Because I really want you to learn something from reading this book, I have included review questions at the end of many of the chapters. Please do not gloss over these questions. Attempting to answer questions is hard work, even if it is pertaining to information you just finished reading. But testing is more than evaluation; it is one of the best tools for learning because it forces you to recall information that your brain wants to forget (Brown, Roediger, & McDaniel, 2014). These review questions are also a good reminder of what I think is most important from each chapter. Welcome to class! Some of the chapters have homework assignments. You should do them because they are for your benefit. And yes, this will be on the test. In fact, this book ends with an Appendix containing a final exam, which is a combination of all the chapter review questions.

The four parts of the research competency model I created from my own research on student affairs professionals—research values, research skills, research behaviors, and research culture—guided the chapters of this book (Sriram, 2014a).

In Chapter 1, I discuss some research that highlights the limitations to human intuition. Applying Nobel Laureate Daniel Kahneman's (2011) work, I emphasize the need to use your logic and reason (student affairs slow) in addition to your instincts (student affairs fast).

Incorporating more research into our work needs to be a team effort. In Chapter 2, I begin with the basics of defining and understanding the concept of *research*. What is it? How does it differ from assessment? (Spoiler alert: I do not believe it does differ from assessment.) Chapter 3 discusses how to develop a research paradigm and the importance of culture in developing it. If you are one of only a few individuals in your division of student affairs who care about how research can help improve student affairs work, all is not lost. But the real power comes from a group of people together awakening to the gift of research in student affairs.

Chapter 4 is where we begin to get our hands dirty by discussing research design. Chapters 5 and 6 cover developing your own surveys to answer your own questions about students on your own campus, as survey development is a topic often lacking in most research and statistics books. In Chapter 7, I cover basic statistics and try to explain foundational statistical concepts as clearly as I can. Chapters 8 through 11 discuss statistical approaches everyone should know. In this book, I do not tell you how to conduct a multiple regression using statistical software (there are plenty of books that can tell you that). I do, however, explain what a multiple regression is, what it does for you, and what to expect from its results, all while using examples directly related to higher education and student affairs.

Chapter 12 is where I get practical about what I would like to see change as a result of this book. This chapter first discusses change on the individual level. I explain the concept of habits and how developing research habits can transform the quality of your work without adding to the quantity of your work. As I suggest in Chapter 12, I recommend you spend the first 15 minutes of each workday reading this book. Create a habit by walking into your office, setting a timer, and reading for 15 minutes before turning on your computer and checking e-mail. The brain learns best when it sips rather than chugs, and this is not the kind of book you want to read in two or three long sittings. I break the book into smaller chunks with subheadings, so another way to approach this book is to read one subheading each workday.

Chapter 12 also discusses what staff of departments and divisions of student affairs can do together to integrate research into practice. Organizations are transformed when culture is transformed.

It is culture that drives behavior (Schein, 2010), and I dream of higher education departments and entire divisions of student affairs that regularly engage professionals in thinking fast and thinking slow (Kahneman, 2011). It is time we reclaim the *scholar* in scholar practitioner (Sriram & Oster, 2012).

ACKNOWLEDGMENTS

I teach because I want to shape the lives of my students. Oh, but how often they shape me! Years ago, Meghan Oster, a graduate student of mine, challenged me to not just wish student affairs professionals were scholar practitioners but to help them become scholar practitioners. And so began a journey. When Corina Kaul, another graduate student, heard I was writing this book, she offered me the chance to lead a workshop and test the book itself on student affairs professionals. I told her no one would come. I was wrong. I want to thank both of them, as well as the 10 student affairs professionals who participated: Leia Duncan, Terri Garrett, Jeff Strietzel, Chris Kirk, Holly Joyner, Erin Payseur, Dana Lee Haines, Lamar Bryant, Sakina Trevathan, and Sharyl Loeung. I also want to thank other graduate students of mine who have shaped and formed me: Melissa McLevain, Jennifer Perkins, Jared Dauenhauer, Elijah Jeong, Jesse Farley, Ah Ra Cho, and Kerri Bond.

Professionally, three people invested in me to such a great extent I cannot possibly express my gratitude adequately. I want to thank Francis Shushok for the many roles he plays in my life: mentor; encourager; teacher; and, most important, friend. Eileen Hulme, thank you for giving me a vision for what higher education and student affairs can and should be to students. You are an inspiration. Laurie Schreiner, you have a gift for teaching that is profound. Thank you for teaching me how to be a scholar.

I walked into a meeting room at a professional conference, sat down with David Brightman, and pitched the idea for this book. I was frankly astonished at his openness, professionalism, curiosity, and partnership. I feel very fortunate to have you as my editor, David, and I am deeply grateful for how you made this book better. I also want to express thanks to my reviewers and colleagues who were willing to read manuscripts and offer feedback.

Amanda, thank you for the honor of journeying through life with you. You are my favorite, and I apologize in advance for talking about you in this book. I can't help it. Also, thank you for encouraging me to write every day. It made all the difference. Ellis, thank you for letting me teach you how to use statistics at what most would argue is too young an age. Lily, thank you for inviting me to write a book with you. I can't wait until we publish it. Stella, thank you for bringing a spark into my life. Your energy is a joy. Mom and Dad, thank you for your willingness to sacrifice anything and everything for me.

And finally, I want to thank you. Yes, you. You are not only the type of person to read a book like this one (which makes us instant friends) but also the type of person to read the acknowledgments section of a book (which makes me not want to hang out with you). A colleague of mine, Scott Moore, once encouraged me to focus less on making a significant contribution to my field but instead make a significant contribution to people. If I positively contribute to your learning and your work in any way, I am grateful. Thank you for giving me the chance.

INTRODUCTION

I still remember the first day I met Frank Shushok. I was in a master's program in higher education and student affairs, and my program was in the midst of a major transition. Previously, the program had been pieced together in the department of educational administration by combining leadership, counseling, and psychology courses, and weaving in a few courses specifically related to higher education. The program was far from challenging. Although a small part of me wished for more challenge, a larger part of me was thankful for a graduate program I could cruise through while working full-time.

Then came Frank. He had been hired to fill a senior position in the division of student affairs after completing two graduate degrees from notable national programs. It was my second year in the program, and I was taking a new class he created called the Culture and Organization of Higher Education. The title should have given me a clue that something would be different about this class. It didn't, but the first day of class certainly did. I was challenged as never before. I was actually forced to read, and read well. There were weekly reading exams, and the answers required more than regurgitating facts from the books. This class was *hard*. And I loved it. Others did not feel the same way, as you might imagine. In fact, I remember telling Frank in my anonymous written student evaluation to not listen to the negative comments I predicted would come from my classmates. This class was exactly what we needed. Actually, Frank was exactly what we needed.

Frank opened new possibilities for me on how those in student affairs could do their jobs. I started applying for jobs in the institution based on whether the job would give me more time and access to Frank. How did he know so much? How did he so seamlessly shift between using his heart and using his mind? How did he so naturally go between his intuition and his reason? When

I became the director of the first living-learning program on our campus, Frank asked me if I wanted to join him on a research project to evaluate the impact of the program. I did not know you could evaluate the impact of a program. Before long, we developed our own survey, discussed quantitative research methodologies, and learned together about statistical approaches. He did not know everything, but he certainly knew more than I did. His willingness to learn what we needed to know fueled my willingness to learn as well. Eighteen months later, we completed a study comparing engineering students at our institution who participated in our living-learning program to engineering students who did not. We accounted for things like entrance test scores, gender, and race. In time, we had some convincing evidence that the living-learning program was making a meaningful, positive impact on students. I was thrilled and satisfied with that in itself. And when Frank asked if I wanted to try to publish our research, I said yes (Shushok & Sriram, 2010).

Perhaps you have a Frank Shushok in your life—someone who views higher education and student affairs administration as an exercise in the intellect as well as the heart. Someone who, although certainly caring, compassionate, and committed to helping students, made an impression on you because of her or his ability to think. If you do not have someone like that in your professional life, you are missing out. But all is not lost. You can be that person.

Understanding the Research Competency in Student Affairs

When the American College Personnel Association (ACPA) and NASPA–Student Affairs Professionals in Higher Education (2010) joined to publish a common list of competencies in student affairs, it represented good news for the field for several reasons. First, it was nice to see the two largest student affairs professional organizations in the country working together for a common goal. Second, it gave the profession an agreed-on list of overarching skills needed for student affairs work. Third, it brought new meaning to the idea of improving the craft of student affairs. It was one thing to encourage everyone in student affairs to get better, but it was another to give the idea of getting better a specific shape and form.

Given the importance of the student affairs competencies, it surprised me that little had been done to measure competencies in student affairs professionals. I thought I would find a long literature review of research studies examining these competencies. Instead, the early research is not much more than asking people in the field which areas they think they should be competent in. There is nothing wrong with asking student affairs professionals what they think about competencies; it is a good place to start. However, advancements in statistics provide all sorts of tools to measure psychological constructs such as competencies, but these helpful tools were put to little use. Digging through the literature, I did find a few courageous people who attempted to do just that by measuring one specific competency (Castellanos, Gloria, Mayorga, & Salas, 2007; Kuk, Cobb, & Forrest, 2007; Waple, 2006). I also felt it was time, now that we had an official list of competencies, to try to measure all the competencies in as many student affairs professionals as possible. So I did.

When I first thought about measuring the competencies of student affairs professionals, several reasons why I should not be the one to do this came to mind. I did not know enough about the competencies. I did not know enough about statistical measurement. I felt that someone notable in the field should do this kind of notable work. Then I got over it and tried to do it anyway. I learned some wonderful things from this quest. For example, I learned how to create an instrument that measures competencies in student affairs professionals, how to check for validity and reliability, and how to develop models to explain how the competencies may interact and influence one another. I also learned that the competencies in my research discoveries were not exactly the same as the competencies published by ACPA and NASPA. They were close, but the differences fascinated me, especially those that most had to do with the research competency.

The notion of becoming competent in research in student affairs does not quite capture the multifaceted beauty of the research competency. Research in student affairs is better thought of as four smaller competencies (see Figure I.1), subcomponents that fit

Figure I.1. The research competency in student affairs.

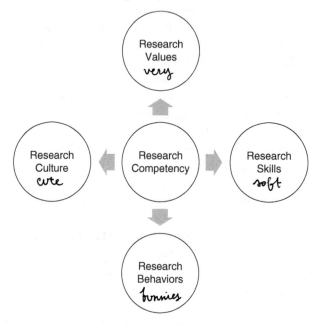

together like puzzle pieces to form something larger, which I named *research values, research skills, research behaviors,* and *research culture* (Sriram, 2014a).

Part of what it means to have the research competency is to value research and its usefulness for student affairs work (research values). As you might imagine, not everyone in student affairs cares about research, sees it as helpful, or wants anything to do with it. You have to care about research to get better at research. Such care goes beyond you as the individual; it extends to the entire division of student affairs on your campus. This is what I mean by research culture. Some divisions of student affairs have cultures that actively, although maybe in hidden ways, discourage engagement in research in student affairs work. Others, some of which I have had the distinct privilege of visiting, have a culture that nudges everyone to be a scholar practitioner, to work in student affairs fast and slow. Possessing individual research values and an organizational research culture are vitally important but seldom discussed. Whether student affairs professionals have the skills to understand, evaluate, and conduct research matters only when the environment is right.

Research skills might just be the elephant in the room in student affairs. Terms like *assessment, statistics, validity,* and *reliability* float around on our campuses, and we know that we should know what they mean. But sometimes we may smile, nod, and do our best to acknowledge the importance of these ideas without exposing our lack of knowledge or inexperience about them. As I mentioned before, you may not have had the chance, based on your background, to learn these skills. Or perhaps you were supposed to learn them, but the courses designed to teach you these skills were not enough. Knowing these terms is about more than sounding smart. If you understand research, you can discern the quality of research others present to you. Even better, you can seek answers to your own important questions in your work. Assessment is of increasing importance in higher education. Student affairs professionals are asked to put research skills to use to demonstrate the effects of their practice. Surprisingly, having research skills and using research skills are two very different things.

The demands placed on student affairs professionals continue to grow. From mental health issues to campus crises to student learning, almost everything that occurs in the lives of college students outside the classroom walls involves student affairs. And in certain areas, such as leadership development, student affairs professionals take an active role in classrooms as well. I understand I cannot change your research behaviors by asking you to add something to a list of responsibilities that is already too long. If we are going to incorporate more research into our work, it must involve how we do our work rather than adding to the volume of work. In my research, I learned that possessing research skills does not necessarily lead to research behaviors. In fact, to find the student affairs professionals who engage in research the most on your campus—from reading research about college students to exploring answers to their own questions—look no further than the graduate students in higher education or student affairs programs who work part-time in graduate assistantships (Sriram & Oster, 2012). If you want to find professionals who engage in research the least, look for student affairs professionals with doctorates. People with doctorates, which usually bring with them senior responsibilities, do not always have research habits associated with their degrees. I think that needs to change.

So when I write about research competency in student affairs, I am referring to research values, research culture, research skills, and research behaviors. We need to make vast improvements in all four areas, and this book is meant to help in all four areas, which serve as the learning outcomes for the book.

I

STUDENT AFFAIRS, FAST AND SLOW

Holly is not quite satisfied with the current ways her department in student affairs supports students of color. The purpose of her department is to help underrepresented students. Sometimes she feels it is easier to convince people outside her department that more needs to be done than it is to persuade her own coworkers. Holly loves her coworkers, who love students and care deeply about their mission to increase multicultural competence on campus. When it comes to challenging the assumptions of others outside their department and calling them to do more for students of color, no one does it better than her coworkers. But challenging their own assumptions and accomplishments within the department is a different story.

Holly is a little nervous walking to the conference room for the staff meeting. After some small talk, the meeting is set to begin. Holly starts by expressing appreciation for the countless hours they all devote to making their institution a more inclusive environment where learning can thrive. Her coworkers smile, unaware that they are also slightly nodding in agreement. Carefully avoiding the word *but*, Holly attempts to explain that more can be done by their department to support students who identify as African American or Black. The smiles stop. Her coworkers wait impatiently for their turn, and Holly can sense the increased anxiety. She decides to cut short her comments and listen.

One coworker, feeling defensive, states that he thinks they are doing a lot considering their small staff. He mentions an African

7

American speaker he helped bring to campus two months ago. Students, especially Black students, loved the speaker, he claims. Another coworker brings up a conversation she had the day before with an African American female student who was praising the department for its efforts to make campus life better for all. Yet another coworker, who now feels obliged to enter the conversation, says that this department's efforts for African American students go far beyond the last institution she worked for.

Holly feels stuck. She has anecdotal stories to defend her point of view also but chooses not to use them. She is surrounded by great professionals, but she wants more for them; she wants to challenge them as well as support them. She thinks to herself, "Isn't there more we can do to evaluate a problem than merely discussing how we feel about it?"

The Power of Intuition

Perhaps no book brings to light the power of intuition and experience better than Malcolm Gladwell's (2005) *Blink: The Power of Thinking Without Thinking*. Humans are beautiful creatures, and their intuition is an amazing gift, but it can be underappreciated. Decisions made through intuition can be impressively accurate and fast. In his book, Gladwell discusses the relatively new notion of the adaptive unconscious, something in our brain comparable to a powerful computer with enormous storage capacity that discreetly processes data and comes to conclusions about problems, solutions, and actions. When we think of ourselves, we think of our conscious selves. The truth is that we can and do switch between our conscious and unconscious modes of thinking depending on the context and need of the current situation.

An important aspect of intuition is "thin-slicing" (Gladwell, 2005, p. 23), which occurs when our unconscious minds find patterns and meaning in situations based on small moments, or slices, of experience. Everyone has this ability. First impressions are a perfect example of thin-slicing. We create positive or negative judgments about people only minutes after meeting them, and these impressions can be surprisingly accurate and insightful. I see student affairs professionals thin-slicing with students frequently. They are able to detect that something is wrong in a student's life—that a student needs additional attention and care—even if they cannot explain how they know.

Part of improving the decisions we make is to pay proper tribute to the mysterious nature of our intuitive judgments. Sometimes it is possible to know something without knowing why or how you know it. The brain is a powerful tool that you will often use without knowing how you are using it or even that you are using it. In addition to intuition, another term we use for this type of thinking is *habit*. More than 40% of our actions stem from habits instead of conscious decisions (Duhigg, 2012). With habits, the brain simplifies a sequence of actions into one automatic routine, a process known as *chunking*. What the brain once looked at as a series of steps, it now perceives as one step. This is similar to how a person learning to read might see a series of letters, while an experienced reader only sees one complete word, thus gaining efficiency from simplicity.

Habits form because the brain constantly wants to find ways to save energy (Duhigg, 2012). Intuition is an important time saver. We cannot always gather all the data, analyze all the facts, and wait for the right decision to appear. Stories, anecdotes, and experiences can all be thin slices, moments that tell you much more than what can be seen in the moment itself.

So what about my opening example with Holly? Couldn't her coworkers be thin-slicing in their reaction to her? How does Holly know that their anecdotes and feelings were not accurate representations of reality, packaged in an energy-saving, time-efficient manner? She does not know. What she does know is that as powerful as intuition can be, it is also fallible. Our intuition has limitations, or blind spots. And for this reason, we need logic.

The Limits of Intuition and the Power of Reason

Gladwell's (2005) objective in *Blink* is to highlight the power of intuition. He is also the first to admit, however, that intuition has its limits: "Our unconscious is a powerful force. But it's fallible. It's not the case that our internal computer always shines through, instantly decoding the 'truth' of a situation. It can be thrown off, distracted, and disabled" (p. 15). As Levitt and Dubner (2014) explain, conventional wisdom is usually wrong. Humans are too easily persuaded by anecdotal evidence, adhere to beliefs that are often mistaken, and are overly confident about their ability to draw conclusions that accurately describe the world (Nisbett, 2015).

But let's face it: Intuition is easy. We want to believe we can be successful professionals in student affairs by relying on our unconscious, behind-the-scenes thinking. Constantly relying on intuition and experience is a big mistake, however. It puts you in a place where you are likely to make wrong decisions, and you then feel pressured to defend your decisions. To defend your decisions, you unconsciously pay attention only to the evidence that supports your decisions, ignoring the facts that prove you wrong. This is known as *confirmation bias*; that is, people are biased toward information that confirms what they already believe. Research finds that even very intelligent people look for evidence to confirm their beliefs while ignoring any information to the contrary (Levitt & Dubner, 2014). How do we overcome this fallibility of intuition?

This is where the skills of logic and reason come in.

Richard Nisbett (2015), a psychologist who has served as a distinguished professor at the University of Michigan, wrote a book that represents the other end of the spectrum from Gladwell's (2005) *Blink*. In *Mindware*, Nisbett's goal is to bring to light the power of logic and reason in thinking. Logic, he writes, is abstract, formal, and central to Western thought. Dialectical reasoning, logic's counterpart, constitutes principles for deciding about the truth and is central to Eastern thought. Psychologists, economists, statisticians, logicians, and philosophers, beginning with Socrates in the Western tradition, have developed tools to shape thinking, which are concepts, principles, and rules of inference.

Reason can be divided into two categories: deductive reasoning and inductive reasoning (Nisbett, 2015). Deductive reasoning is represented in formal logic, a set of abstract rules for drawing conclusions. It begins with theories or premises and ends with examples or facts that demonstrate those premises. An example of deductive reasoning is the syllogism, a type of logic that is illustrated in the following famous example: All humans are mortal. Socrates is a human. Therefore, Socrates is mortal. Venn diagrams are a type of visual syllogism. Another example of deductive reasoning is conditional logic: If A, then B. Inductive reasoning, in contrast to deductive reasoning, begins with examples or facts and uses them to build up to a theory or premise. Inductive reasoning is exemplified in the scientific method.

Why is logic important? Because it can help to overcome the fallibility of intuition. When data are available, data are helpful. And gathering data to inform a problem is almost always feasible. As Ian Ayres (2007) writes: "We are in a historic moment of horse-versus-locomotive competition, where intuitive and experiential expertise is losing out time and time again to number crunching" (p. 10). Ayres observes that people think they know more than they actually do, which leads not only to biased predictions but also to overconfidence in those biased predictions. This is true even when it comes to first impressions, an example I used to discuss the power of intuition. Psychologists have a term—*fundamental attribution error*—for when we make conclusions about a person's personality on only one or two observations. Instead of thinking the person is mean, perhaps he or she had a bad day. Instead of thinking the person is shy, perhaps you said something that offended him or her. We need logic and reason to prevent these kinds of mistakes. In fact, in a series of experiments, Ayres (2007) and others found that statistical equations repeatedly beat out experts in making accurate predictions. And the results were not close.

Thinking, Fast and Slow

So, in one corner, we have Gladwell (2005) helping you to understand that intuition is a powerful and fast tool that should be embraced rather than ignored. In another corner, we have authors like Nisbett (2015) and Ayres (2007) helping you understand the importance of logic and reason over and above intuition. How do you bring these competing ideas together? What does this mean for student affairs? I think the answer can be found in Nobel Laureate Daniel Kahneman's (2011) excellent work, *Thinking, Fast and Slow.*

Kahneman (2011) describes with depth and clarity two modes of thinking. He refers to one as System 1, thinking fast, which is when your thinking operates automatically and quickly. Thinking fast is your intuition. He calls the other mode of thinking System 2, thinking slow. This is when your thinking requires great attention and effort to solve complex problems. Thinking slow is your logic and reason (Stanovich & West, 2000).

The interplay between the two systems is fascinating. Your thinking-fast system runs automatically, is typically the dominant system, and likes to be in control. Rather than describing your two systems at war with one another, Kahneman (2011) explains that your thinking-slow system actually is happy to concede the battle and likes to operate in standby mode, requiring little mental effort and attention. Only a small part of its capacity is typically engaged.

Your thinking-fast system, by contrast, wants to be the boss of your mind because it makes things easy, effortless, and fast. Your thinking-slow system—logic and reason—also wants your intuition to be the boss of your mind so that it does not have to do the hard work of thinking in an effortful, attention-requiring manner. This is not a good thing. The two systems need to be partners, dancing together to the rhythm of your mind. Letting your thinking-fast system run the show exposes you to biases, systematic errors, and answering easier questions than the ones being asked, all the while ignoring reason, logic, and statistics (Kahneman, 2011). Kahneman's advice is to purposefully use your logic and reason so that it is in balance with your intuition. "The best we can do is a compromise," he writes. "Learn to recognize the situations in which mistakes are likely and try harder to avoid significant mistakes when the stakes are high" (p. 28).

You need your thinking-slow system to step up and play a greater role in your thinking. The good news is that thinking slow—using logic and reason—can be taught. This finding surprised Nisbett (2015), but it became the reason he wrote *Mindware*. Nisbett found that taking college courses on logic, learning statistics, and employing the principles of the scientific method all improve the way people think and solve problems. After the great success of Levitt and Dubner's (2006) *Freakonomics* (2006), they wrote *Think Like a Freak* (2014) to teach others how to approach problem-solving in a fashion similar to their approach. They call this the *economic approach* (Levitt and Dubner are economists, after all), or how to deal with problems by relying on data to understand how the world works. We need to get better at thinking slow, and we can get better at thinking slow. This is good news. But there is more good news.

As it turns out, improving your ability to think slow also improves your intuition.

Gladwell (2005) writes that the most important task of his book is "to convince you that our snap judgments and first impressions can be educated and controlled" (p. 15). First impressions develop from past experiences and the environment. Changing experiences, therefore, changes first impressions. The kinds of thinking you do, the kinds of problems you solve, and the processes you use, all have an impact on your unconscious, thinking-fast intuition. Those who have good instincts were not born with some special gift. The special gift is a result of practice, training, and rehearsal. Thinking slow is good for you not only because it prevents you from making some of the mistakes that result from thinking fast but also because it makes you better (and more accurate) when you think fast. Gladwell explains:

> Our unconscious reactions come out of a locked room, and we can't look inside that room. But with experience we become expert at using our behavior and our training to interpret—and decode—what lies behind our snap judgments and first impressions. (p. 183)

Through understanding how (and when) to think fast and think slow, we develop into better solvers of the problems we face.

Although Ayres (2007) wrote *Super Crunchers* to explain that thinking slow leads to better decisions than thinking fast does, he also insists that using statistics "doesn't mean the end of intuition or the unimportance of on-the-job experience. Rather, we are likely to see a new era where the best and brightest are comfortable with both statistics and ideas" (p. 16). Even if we input data into statistical software for computer analysis, humans are still deciding which variables to input and how to measure those variables. Intuition is vital to interpret the results of data analyses.

Thinking fast generates hypotheses and hunches about cause-and-effect relationships. Thinking slow provides more objective feedback on how variables influence one another. Then, thinking fast decides how to make sense of that feedback and, more important, what actions to take as a result. Thinking fast is a precursor to thinking slow, which then helps you to think fast more accurately. After all, "a marker of skilled performance is the ability to deal with

Figure 1.1. Thinking, fast and slow.

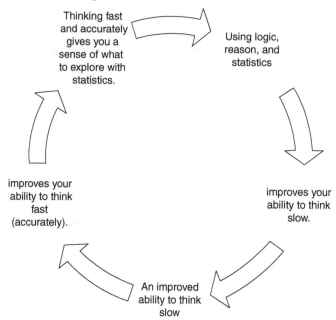

vast amounts of information swiftly and efficiently" (Kahneman, 2011, p. 416). We need to learn when to speed up and when to slow down our thinking. Logic, reason, and statistics slow down our thinking; intuition speeds it up (see Figure 1.1).

Everything is an inference (Nisbett, 2015). Whether you are thin-slicing or number crunching, you are attempting to draw larger conclusions from smaller samples. Everyone who is trying to solve a problem makes an inference. A little more data, a little more information, a little more experience can often lead to better inferences. When you make better inferences, you solve problems better. When you solve problems better, you make the lives of college students better.

Student Affairs, Fast and Slow

This book is about how to do student affairs slow. I know it is counterintuitive, but you must slow down your thinking in our increasingly complex, fast-paced environments. In his book on assessment in student affairs, Schuh (2009) states that accountability is an essential dimension in contemporary student affairs practice. He also acknowledges that few people enter student affairs because they want to conduct assessment. Nevertheless, Schuh asserts that research skills are a necessity, not a luxury. In their Documenting Effective Educational Practice project, Kuh, Kinzie, Schuh, and Whitt (2010) found that data-informed decision-making was part of the organizational habits of improvement-oriented institutions. If we cannot assume that one or two research methods courses alone will develop these needed quantitative skills in students, then "it is imperative that senior student affairs leaders make sure that in-service experiences are available for staff so that they can keep their skills in this area sharp and contemporary" (p. 243). In other words, research skills come from conducting research in practice. Professionals need to know how to design a study, collect data, analyze data, interpret results, and present the results in an understandable manner (Schuh, 2009). This is student affairs fast and student affairs slow working together harmoniously.

Looking back, scholars of student affairs have called on professionals to use student affairs slow since almost the beginning of the field. Evans and Reason (2001) observe that beginning with the American Council on Education's (1949) *Student Personnel Point of View*, authors of all the philosophical statements that guide the profession of student affairs advocated "an intentional approach to student affairs work" (p. 372). In the early years of the twentieth century, William Raney Harper (1905) called for the "scientific study of the student" (p. 321). These statements further explain that intentionality requires grounding in theory and research.

You have a choice. Choosing to primarily rely on thinking fast in your work is the most common option. Blimling (2011) observes that programs can and will operate regardless of how well practitioners incorporate research and theory into their work, and some of these programs will be successful. But he also adds that research and theory help professionals know why programs work or don't and can empower scholar practitioners to evaluate, improve, and create better experiences for college students. Thinking slow helps you know why something works, and knowing why is powerful (Broido, 2011). Therefore, thinking slow is what "separates the professional from the amateur" (Blimling, 2011, p. 49). Allen (2002) goes so far as to call these kinds of professionals "gifted practitioners in student affairs" (p. 152).

Student affairs slow also requires a willingness to accept results that are different from what was wanted or expected. Young (2001) said scholar practitioners must at times choose between loyalty to the truth or to the institution. I think Young would agree that being loyal to the truth is being loyal to the institution but not in the way administrators in the institution may desire. Scholar practitioners must be free to explore controversial ideas and share what they find, no matter what they find (Young, 2001). Divisions of student affairs administrators can and should encourage a culture of data-driven decision-making that expects and rewards thinking slow through the use of logic and reason (Schroeder & Pike, 2001).

Gladwell (2005) argues that the best decisions come from a balancing act between deliberate and instinctive thinking.

> Deliberate thinking [thinking slow] is a wonderful tool when we have the luxury of time, the help of a computer, and a clearly defined task, and the fruits of that type of analysis can set the stage for rapid cognition [thinking fast]. (p. 141)

Blimling (2011) writes, "Knowledge of theory in student affairs [student affairs slow] helps student affairs professionals develop the habits of the mind [student affairs fast] that define how to think about the educational needs of students" (p. 47). Our field needs professionals who know how to do student affairs fast and slow.

So how do you get there? Quantitative research and statistics is not the only way, but it is a good way to teach student affairs professionals how to think slow. Nisbett (2015) discovered that studying statistical principles can have big effects on people's ability to use reason. Thinking by numbers is a tool that provides some objectivity to your analysis. The numbers are there, but you must still interpret them. This book is not about getting you to publish, it is not about getting professionals to act more like faculty. This book is about helping student affairs professionals—scholar practitioners—think slow to provide better programs, policies, and places for students.

Our current ways of operating are not sufficient. Our students need more, and they deserve better. Student affairs professionals are known to be doers and feelers. But we also need student affairs professionals who are known for their thinking. Their slow thinking. Quantitative research is not only a tool that allows you to make better decisions but also a way to teach your mind to think differently. By learning quantitative research and statistics, you are taking another step to form yourself as a scholar practitioner who is better equipped to serve college students. I want to help you get there.

Review Questions From This Chapter

Use the following review questions to test yourself. When you test yourself, you force yourself to recall information, and the act of recalling leads to better and deeper learning.

- What does it mean to think fast?
- What does it mean to think slow?
- How can you learn to think slow more often in your work in student affairs?

2

AN INTRODUCTION
TO RESEARCH

Chris is two years into his first entry-level position in a division of student affairs. He has had a great start. Chris is conscientious, hardworking, and receives feedback well. He cares deeply about his job, and he has performed above expectations since his first report card in grade school. Around campus, Chris is known for his dependability. He is always on time, and he seems to somehow always be on top of his e-mail. In his first two annual reviews, Chris received high praise from his supervisor. And yet, Chris is feeling dissatisfied. He is not being challenged, and he does not really want to be known as the person who always answers e-mails promptly. He wants to be known for his ability to engage in hard thinking to solve complex problems. Chris wants to be challenged. As proactive as he tends to be, Chris wonders how he can contribute in more meaningful ways by incorporating research into his work.

An Introduction to Research

Chapter 1 discussed what it means to think fast, and how you also need to think slow in student affairs. It is now time to lay a foundation of knowledge regarding research.

Research is a word that is used a lot in academia. But what exactly is it? This chapter provides an overview of research, presenting key concepts in an understandable manner. Interestingly, the *Publication*

Manual of the American Psychological Association (American Psychological Association, 2010) does not define *research*. It begins with the assumption that you know what research is. And you probably do. Sort of. But how would you define it?

I define *research* by breaking the word into its two parts: *re* and *search*. Let's start with *search*. Research is the search for truth. When you examine all scholars in all disciplines, you find different ways of viewing the world, different terminology, and different cultures. But what all scholars have in common is an ongoing search for truth. Scholars want to know the truth about what Shakespeare's plays mean, the truth about how to cure cancer. Scholars want to know the truth about how to improve education. We all have opinions. We all have theories. We also all want to know the truth.

But no one can discover the truth on one's own. No one begins from square one. This is where the *re* part of research comes in. Research is not just the search for truth; it is the search for truth based on other people's search for truth. It would be arrogant (and downright stupid) to embark on a search for truth while ignoring everything everyone else has done to discover truth before you. We think of innovation as original, but innovation is incremental. It is the incremental improvement on other people's improvements. Eventually, these small improvements lead to a breakthrough (Ericsson & Pool, 2016). To repeat, research is the search for truth based on other people's search for truth.

As a student affairs professional, you want to know the truth. There are two main ways to get to truth: analyzing ideas and analyzing data. When scholars analyze ideas, they present the ideas of other scholars then compare, contrast, integrate, and synthesize those ideas, concluding with their own new ideas about the truth. When scholars analyze data, they do so by collecting data numerically (quantitative research) or through words (qualitative research). *Empirical research* is a general term to describe research based on collected data. Quantitative research is the focus of this book, but this type of research is not superior or inferior to qualitative research. They are completely different (and therefore complementarily helpful) approaches to searching for truth. We need both. I cannot imagine a research quest that would not be helped by having rigorous quantitative, qualitative, and theoretical approaches to

Figure 2.1. Initial scaffold for understanding research.

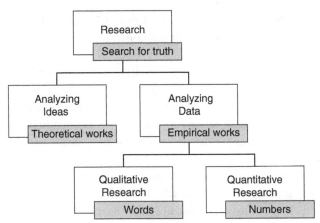

discovering truth. Figure 2.1 provides an initial scaffold for understanding research.

What truth do student affairs professionals want to know? Several examples come to mind. Many relevant questions can be summarized by asking, Does it make a difference? Do our programs, policies, and places influence students, and if so, which students and in what ways? Many divisions of student affairs offer optional orientation camps for incoming first-year students, and many divisions see value in students living on campus. Many divisions have departments of multiculturalism that offer particular programs and services. Do these programs work? If so, for whom do they work? White students? African Americans? Men? Women? First-year students? Seniors? These are some of the questions student affairs professionals need to answer because answering them leads to a better experience for college students. You can put more resources into the programs that work, modify or stop the programs that don't, and better understand which students are being reached and in what ways (and which students are not being reached and what can be done to reach them). In an era of high tuition costs and limited resources, you cannot afford to simply feel good about the work you do without some objective feedback. You need to know the truth. And this brings me to the question, How do you know the truth? How do you know what you know?

Understanding Epistemologies

Epistemology is the study of knowledge. A branch of philosophy focused on how we know what we know, it is concerned with the nature and standards of knowledge (Vogt & Johnson, 2011). Creswell (2014), a notable teacher of research design, describes epistemology as a philosophical worldview. An epistemology is important because it informs the research methodology or approach. There are several epistemologies, but in an attempt to keep a balance between simplicity and complexity, I discuss two major ones: constructivism and postpositivism.

Constructivism is an epistemology formalized by Swiss psychologist Jean Piaget (Wadsworth, 1996). Through his research on children, Piaget theorized that humans learn by constructing their knowledge from their experiences (Vogt & Johnson, 2011). Important works in formalizing constructivism include those of Berger and Luekmann (1967) and Lincoln and Guba (1985). Constructivism is the basis for qualitative research, which often uses interviews to understand how people create meaning and knowledge from what they experience. This meaning-making is central to the human experience, and the constructivist researcher will often look for and appreciate a complexity of views rather than try to simplify views by arranging them into larger categories (Creswell, 2014). The constructivist researcher discovers truth by relying heavily on the participants' views of a situation. Therefore, the questions asked are broad, general, and open ended. Constructivism also acknowledges that context, culture, and relationships will influence how humans construct meaning. *Constructivism* and *constructionism* are terms sometimes used interchangeably, but Crotty (2003) distinguishes between the two by describing constructivism as individual meaning-making and constructionism as cultural meaning-making (i.e., social constructionism).

Similar to how constructivism influences qualitative research methodologies, postpositivism influences quantitative research. (This is an oversimplification but a helpful one to start.) Positivism is the basis for the scientific method. With a positivist epistemology, researchers originally believed in the absolute truth of all knowledge and in our ability to perfectly understand that truth. This was the ultimate form of objectivism—the view that reality and meaning exist apart from anyone's consciousness. Crotty (2003) uses the example of a tree in a forest. The tree is a tree, regardless of how you feel about it. It does not need you or anyone else for it to be a tree. Since then, scholars have distanced themselves from such extreme views about facts and reality. Postpositivism pulls back from the extreme claims of positivism by a desire to understand truth factually while also admitting that error and imperfection will always be involved (Creswell, 2014).

Postpositivists are fascinated by cause-and-effect relationships. Researchers in this epistemology desire to test, experiment, and examine relationships among variables. The reason we have gone from positivism to postpositivism is that scientists actively construct scientific knowledge rather than objectively state the laws of the natural world. For example, is that thing in the forest a tree or is it wood? Well, it is both, depending on the context of what you mean. Therefore, even in the search for objective truth, what people think and how they make sense of information matters. We make mistakes and we learn, even when dealing with objective facts. But in the end, postpositivists believe in objective truth and want to accurately discover it. Figure 2.2 adds epistemology to our initial research scaffold.

Epistemology is important, but it is not often discussed in conversations about research. In the latest articles in higher education and student affairs, the researchers do not directly state their epistemology. Research is the search for truth based on other people's search for truth; epistemology is how you think about discovering truth. Some believe they discover truth by constructing meaning from experience (constructivism). Others believe that truth is already out there, in existence, without our meaning-making (postpositivism). One perspective is subjective, and the other is objective. But both are helpful and needed.

Other epistemologies fall in between constructivism and postpositivism. And some epistemologies come from different perspectives altogether. But I think it's helpful to begin with an understanding of constructivism (and how it ties to qualitative research) and postpositivism (and how it contributes to quantitative research). We need both epistemologies, and it is almost impossible to not draw from both epistemologies in any research study. But a researcher will predominantly draw from one or the other in a given study.

Figure 2.2. Research scaffold with epistemology added.

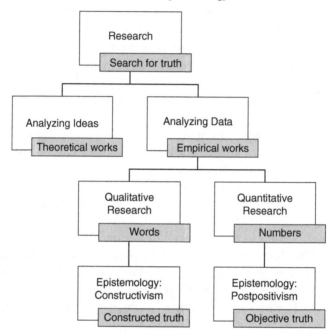

Theory

The term *theory to practice* is frequently used in the literature discussing scholar practitioners (Blimling, 2011). A theory, simply put, is a way of explaining things. We all have theories, and we all use theories. The difference for scholar practitioners is that they use theory deliberately, use multiple theories, and allow theory to help them become more sophisticated thinkers (Evans & Guido, 2012; Love, 2012). As Robert Birnbaum (1988) states, "I believe that the only thing more useful to an administrator than a good theory is several good theories—particularly if they happen to be in conflict with one another" (p. xvi). Frank Shushok (2016) invites readers of *About Campus* to complicate themselves by complicating their thinking. Theory, when used appropriately, is a great way to think slow in student affairs.

A theory is an idea for "how some part of the world works" (Vogt & Johnson, 2011, p. 398). Often, a theory will explain how different variables relate to each other and revolves around the questions of how and why. I once had a graduate student who was taking a class on teaching and learning. As an assignment for the course, the student had to observe two different professors. When the student came to my class to observe me, she took notes furiously. After the class was over, I approached her and asked for her insights and feedback on my teaching. She commented on how much I talk about theory in my class, trying to connect it to practical problems that my graduate students will face (or are currently facing) as student affairs professionals. I smiled and said something like, "Theory is everything." She remarked that the other professor she had observed was antitheory. I dismissed that idea, assuring her that the other professor was not antitheory but rather probably not as deliberately outspoken about theory. To my surprise, she responded that the other professor told his students that he was antitheory. When she used the term *antitheory*, she was quoting him. That anecdote made me sad for two reasons. First, no one is antitheory. We all have ways of explaining things, and we all operate from these theories, consciously or subconsciously. Second, a professor who tells students he is antitheory sends a clear message that theory is useless and a waste of time. That is not what will help develop the future leaders of the world.

You use theory more than you may realize in your work in student affairs. The whole field of student affairs is based on the foundational theory that what happens outside the classroom walls matters to college students. It matters for their grades, whether they stay at the institution, for their personal well-being, their holistic growth, and their learning. That is a theory. It is a way of explaining things. If you believe living on campus is good for college students, you are using a theory. If you believe that some type of campus orientation program is important for students in transition, you are using a theory. If you believe that transfer students have different needs and wants from traditional first-year students, you are using a theory. If you believe anything, you are using a theory. Beliefs are theories. And beliefs are important, because beliefs drive behaviors.

In a great discussion about student affairs fast and slow, Patrick Love (2012) argues for the importance of student affairs fast, which he refers to as using informal theories.

> Many experienced practitioners have a fairly well-deserved repu-
> tation of being antitheory (Strange & King, 1990). Strange and
> King (1990) attributed such mistrust of theory (what you know)
> to the threat it posed for practitioners (people who have done),
> where experience and maturity are so highly valued. I also argue
> that some of the mistrust is because professionals often feel forced
> to choose between formal theory [student affairs slow] and their
> own informal theories [student affairs fast]. (p. 178)

Love advocates for more respect and acknowledgment of informal
theories in student affairs practice (student affairs fast). Evans and
Guido (2012), on the other hand, defend the importance of formal
theory (student affairs slow).

> Overall, we have no issue with the use of informal theory [student
> affairs fast] as a mediator between formal theory [student
> affairs slow] and practice. We do have an issue with using
> informal theory by itself to guide practice, given that it is impos-
> sible to determine the accuracy of an individual's assumptions or
> sense making. Using formal theory as a corrective helps to ensure
> that a practitioner's actions are effective and proactive in nature.
> (p. 199)

So theory is everything. But by *theory*, I mean the deliberate formal theories that make up thinking slow and the intuitive informal
theories that make up thinking fast. These ways of thinking must
complement and build on one another in student affairs practice.

Some of the theories most important to our work are profoundly
simple but nonetheless helpful. Astin (1984) presented the theory
of student involvement, explaining that the more students involved
themselves in the life of the campus, the better they would do in
a number of areas. Tinto (1993) theorized that the key to helping
students persist was to get them integrated into the academic and
social communities of colleges. When you read these theories, you
may be underwhelmed because they seem so obvious. But they were
not obvious to everyone (and still are not), and they certainly had
not been articulated in such thoughtful ways before. When people
articulate theories, they present ideas, and when they do so in writing, it allows serious discussion on the merit of the ideas. Publication

of theory forces us to either agree with the theory (and therefore act on it) or disagree with the theory (and therefore defend why we disagree and offer another theory in its place). Such conversations foster thinking slow in your work, but only when you take the time to engage in these conversations. If you dismiss them because you have work to do, you are dismissing one of the most important aspects of your work.

An interesting characteristic of a theory is that it does not need to be true to be a theory. An idea is an idea, regardless of its accuracy. So just because a theory is a way of explaining things, that does not mean it is a true way of explaining things. Therefore, a key question regarding any theory is, What evidence exists to support the theory? How do you know that the theory you hold on a particular matter captures reality? Is it just how you feel? Is it something you have repeatedly observed? Is it something you have been taught by others and have assumed to be true yourself? These are crucial questions. If you question the evidence supporting your theories, you open yourself to question the theories themselves. And when you question your own theories, you engage in a sophisticated thinking-slow kind of thinking. You complicate yourself (Shushok, 2016).

A scholar practitioner must be willing to question and change theories. How you gather data to inform the validity of your theory depends on your epistemology. Constructivists emphasize data that are gathered through words, interviews, and meaning-making. Post-positivists focus on measurement. This book focuses on quantitative research and, therefore, also uses a postpositivist epistemology. The tried-and-true postpositivist format for discovering truth that leads to theories is the scientific method.

The Scientific Method

There is nothing magical about the scientific method. It represents a series of steps to gather data in a somewhat objective manner. These data can help determine relationships among variables, especially cause-and-effect relationships. In the scientific method, you form questions and then test the answers. There are several steps to the scientific method, and the actual number of steps may vary depending on who is describing them. I describe the scientific method as a seven-step process.

Step 1: Observe. The scientific method begins by noticing something. This noticing should lead to curiosity: What is going on here in our residence halls?

Step 2: Question. These observations lead to more formal questions: Is there some difference between the experiences and outcomes of students who live on campus and those who do not?

Step 3: Hypothesize. When you create a hypothesis, you make a guess about how things might turn out. Discovering truth can be more authentic when you make an honest prediction about what that truth might be: I think students who live on campus are more successful in their academic pursuits than those who do not live on campus.

Step 4: Test. It is time to set up your study and gather the necessary data to make informed conclusions. For example, I am going to try to find two groups that are as equal as possible in terms of entrance test scores, high school grade point average (GPA), and some demographic characteristics. I am then going to test and see if the group that lives on campus has a better GPA or better retention rate than the group that does not live on campus.

Step 5: Analyze. Using established methods, the next step is to analyze your data. In quantitative research, this may mean inputting the data into statistical software and performing various calculations. If qualitative, this may mean finding patterns in the transcriptions of interviews that can be categorized into larger themes of how people are making sense of the world around them: I am going to use statistics to compare the first-year GPA of students who live on campus to students who do not live on campus.

Step 6: Theorize. Even when data are analyzed correctly, the data do not tell you what they mean. You must interpret the results and draw conclusions. Otherwise, what is the point of the research? You did not set out to discover data, you set out to discover truth. What is that truth: How can this set of data give me a new way of explaining to what extent living on campus might influence student success?

Step 7: Teach. There is too much to know and not enough time to know it. Scholar practitioners must learn collectively. No one has time to study everything, so you can study the things you are interested in and learn from what others study. But that only works if you share what you learn and they share what they learn. A vital part of research is sharing your knowledge, whether in an internal report, publication, or presentation: Now that I know that students who live on campus at our institution have higher GPAs than those who do not live on campus, I need to share this with our senior administrators and other colleagues to see how we can create more opportunities for students to live on campus. Figure 2.3 adds the scientific method to our research scaffold.

Figure 2.3. Adding the scientific method to the research scaffold.

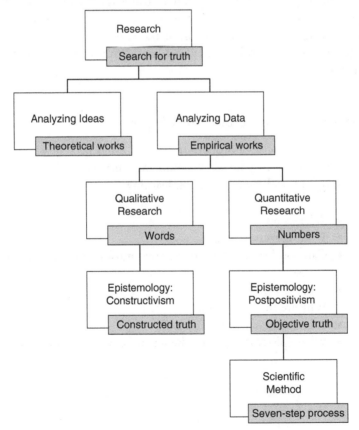

Conclusion

Engaging in research means embarking on a search for truth based on other people's search for truth. You want to discover something new and real, but you also intend to use other people's previous discoveries as a springboard. There are two major philosophies concerning how we go about knowing truth. One foundational epistemology is constructivism, which focuses on the meaning-making processes that people go through to make sense of the world around them. Another foundational epistemology is postpositivism, which emphasizes rational, objective thinking drawn from data collected through measurement. It is helpful to connect constructivism to qualitative research and postpositivism to quantitative research, but any given researcher using any given method may draw from either epistemology (or both). Postpositivism uses the scientific method, which is a series of steps and principles regarding how to go about discovering truth. Discoveries from the scientific method help to inform theories, that is, ways of explaining and making sense of a phenomena.

Review Questions From This Chapter

Use the following review questions to test yourself. When you test yourself, you force yourself to recall information, and the act of recalling leads to better and deeper learning.

- What is research?
- What is epistemology?
- Can you list and describe the two most common epistemologies?
- What is a theory?
- Why are theories useful?
- What is the scientific method?
- What epistemology does the scientific method come from?

3

DEVELOPING A
RESEARCH PARADIGM

Corina was sitting in a university-wide committee meeting concerning the persistence of first-year students to their second year. She served in an assistant director role in the residence life department, and she listened intently as other faculty and staff in the room expressed their ideas for what needs to be done to increase the first-year retention rate. Presently, their campus did not have a policy requiring any students to live on campus. But from Corina's experience, it seemed as if the students who lived on campus were able to make the transition to college life better than those who lived off campus. It was just a hunch (student affairs fast), but Corina wondered if there might be something to it (student affairs slow). Finally, she spoke up: "I get the sense that students who live on campus persist at a higher rate than comparable students who choose not to live on campus. Perhaps I could do some research on whether something is going on there." A female faculty member from the history department began to shake her head. "I do research. You are a staff person. You conduct assessment," she insisted. Corina was dumbfounded. She did not mean to push any buttons, and the faculty member seemed to be missing Corina's main point. But Corina decided to remain silent and let the meeting roll forward.

A Research Paradigm

Scholar practitioners in student affairs need a research paradigm. A paradigm is a mental model that guides our thinking (and eventually our behaviors). Therefore, student affairs professionals need a mental model that includes research to guide their thinking and behaviors. Research is challenging. Research is engaging. Research is a way to make a contribution to your team in a meaningful way. A research paradigm allows a professional to ask questions others are either afraid to ask or not reflective enough to ask. It then propels you to discover truth regarding your questions. The truth will be conditional; it will be incomplete. But it will be truth nonetheless, and truth is how you get better.

A research paradigm means becoming an explorer in your work, not just being an e-mail responder. Most jobs in higher education and student affairs require master's degrees because the work is meant to require high-level thinking. But the logistical and organizational requirements of the job can overshadow the parts that require hard thinking. The fast-paced work will push you toward becoming reactive rather than proactive. Reactive work means spending your time on urgent crises, large and small. Proactive work requires protecting your time so that you can be curious. It means finding the space for important work that is not urgent at all. It takes courage to spend time doing work that no one is directly asking you to do. But such work will lead to a better experience for college students. A research paradigm is not only more fun but also the type of work that we desperately need in the Information Age.

Critical thinking is at the heart of a research paradigm. Critical thinking is based on evidence or sound reasoning. When you use a research paradigm, you engage in thinking slow (Kahneman, 2011). You form your theories—your ways of explaining things—from evidence that you gather or that is gathered by others. And when the evidence does not align with your current mental model, you refine your mental model. Quantitative research and statistics are wonderful tools for gathering and analyzing data, but they are not the only tools that can be used for this purpose (e.g., qualitative research), and they can also certainly be used poorly. But when used correctly, statistics are powerful, not just for the numbers you get, but for the way analyzing the numbers shapes your mental models and your behaviors (your paradigm).

There Is No Such Thing as a Math Brain

One of the biggest obstacles to learning statistics is fear—fear of feeling stupid, fear of not understanding. I used to believe that some people were born with math brains, which were wired in certain ways that allowed them to learn and apply mathematical skills better than I could. This theory took a lot of pressure off me. After all, if these others were born a certain way that was distinctly different from me, what could I do about it?

The problem with my theory is that it was wrong. Completely wrong. After spending years studying expertise and talent, I have come to the conclusion that there is no such thing as a math brain, at least not according to research (Blackwell, Trzesniewski, & Dweck, 2007; Dweck, 2006; Ericsson & Pool, 2016). Our brains learn what we teach them. I no longer believe there are significant, innate differences in people's ability to learn. If my theory is true, then why are there such great differences among people's knowledge, skills, and abilities? I think these differences can be explained through what I call the Five Ms: mind-set, myelin, mastery, motivation, and mentorship.

Mind-set. In the first week of my first class in my PhD program, Eileen Hulme, who served in the roles of professor, mentor, and friend, lent me her copy of Carol Dweck's (2006) book in which she recounts decades of research conducted by her and others showing that people's implicit theories of their abilities have profound consequences on their cognitive processes and behaviors. Put more simply, what you believe about yourself and your potential powerfully affects you. Dweck presents two theories of self: a fixed mind-set and a growth mind-set. Those with a fixed mind-set believe their abilities are fixed and unchangeable. Those with a growth mind-set believe their abilities can be expanded and improved through effort and experience.

These theories are primarily unconscious. For example, if you have a fixed mind-set of intelligence, you believe that people are born with a certain amount of intelligence, and there is not much anyone can do to significantly change. But you do not walk around consciously aware of this theory. Instead, it is an underlying theory that hangs out in the backstage areas of your mind but still powerfully influences your thoughts and actions. A person with a fixed mind-set of intelligence will react to a low grade on a test by either believing he or she is stupid or that the test was unfair. Neither of these reactions is helpful. By contrast, a person with a growth mind-set of intelligence will react to a low grade on a test by questioning the amount of studying he or she did or wondering if there are other methods of study that could be more effective. The reaction leads to empowerment, which leads to the necessary changes for success.

The consequences of the two mind-sets are more important than the mind-sets themselves. Those with a fixed mind-set tend to avoid challenges because challenges test their very self-worth (Dweck, 2006). When they do face challenges and encounter setbacks, these setbacks are detrimental. Failures are interpreted as judgments on their core abilities (because they believe abilities are fixed). So they then ignore any feedback that could help them improve and consider feedback useless because they do not believe they can change. Feedback only pours salt on the wound.

Perhaps the most important consequence of a fixed mind-set is that the person sees effort as a sign of weakness. Do you remember someone from high school (or perhaps it was you) who bragged not only of the high grade he or she received on a test but also of how little studying was done to receive that high grade? This is a telltale sign of a fixed mind-set; accomplishments are even more special when they are achieved with little effort.

The consequences of the growth mind-set are reversed, however. Those with a growth mind-set embrace challenges, view setbacks as temporary, desire to learn from feedback, and place great emphasis on making an effort toward improvement. A growth mind-set leads to healthier responses.

Do you have a fixed mind-set regarding quantitative research and statistics? If so, you are losing the race before you begin. You need to have a growth mind-set for the material in this book, and the point of Dweck's (2006) research is that you can change from a fixed to a growth mind-set. You can counteract your self-talk, respond to failures differently, and begin to believe in your potential for significant change. You must have a growth mind-set for statistics to learn statistics. Nobody learns statistics easily, and if others appear to learn it easily, it is because of all the effort and energy they put into learning math and logic previously. But they are not better or smarter than you. They really aren't. Others may be farther down the proverbial road, but that is a silly reason for you to feel discouraged to start taking steps. A growth mind-set is important because it lays the proper psychological foundation for you to learn. Once you have that foundation, you are ready to understand the neuroscience of learning. Specifically, you need to understand the importance of some white stuff in your brain called myelin.

Myelin. Neurons are cells that are found in your brain and spinal cord. When you learn something, these brain cells connect to one another, forming synapses. Neurons and synapses form the gray matter of your brain, and for a long time this gray matter was the focus of study for neurologists. After all, if this is how learning occurs, then what else really matters? More recently, however, neurologists have turned their attention from the gray matter in the brain to the white matter. It turns out that this white matter, long considered unimportant, serves a vital role in learning, talent, and ability (Fields, 2008).

Neurologists refer to the brain's white matter as myelin. Although synapses do the thinking, myelin acts as a type of insulation for those connections. The more myelin, the faster, stronger, and better the signals of your brain function (Fields, 2008). Forming synapses is not the only important facet of learning. Insulating those signals is how that learning deepens. No one is born with "statistics synapses." Those synapses form when you learn statistics. And no one is born with myelination (insulation) around those statistics synapses. Myelin forms when you repeatedly study and practice statistics. Assuming we are only including healthy brains, the idea that some brains form synapses better than others is foolish at worst and lacks evidence at best. The idea that some brains form myelin better than other brains is also unfounded. The Chinese language Mandarin has a reputation as the most difficult language to learn. It is also the most spoken language in the world. How can that be? Because children who grow up learning and practicing

Mandarin have no trouble forming Mandarin synapses and insulating those signals with myelin. In other words, myelin forms from mastery.

Mastery. The ability to understand and apply quantitative research and statistics is a talent—a skill to be mastered. There are numerous theories regarding talent, and a fixed mind-set—the belief that talent is an innate ability you are born with—is probably the most prevalent theory. But is such a theory informed by research? You may be surprised to learn that there are scholars who devote their energies specifically to the study of talent. The leading scholar in this area is Anders Ericsson, who has numerous publications, but one study in particular was groundbreaking. Ericsson, Krampe, and Tesch-Romer's (1993) article in *Psychological Review* tore down the idea that talent is innate while also laying a foundation for the notion that talent, and perhaps all talent, is developed through what they termed *deliberate practice.*

Deliberate practice consists of effortful activities designed to improve performance. It distinguishes itself from typical practice because it is not just doing the activity; it is doing it in a particular way that focuses on getting better at it. This type of activity requires more attention and more effort, thereby making it more exhausting and even less enjoyable (Ericsson & Pool, 2016). Ericsson and colleagues (1993) wrote, "Many characteristics once believed to reflect innate talent are actually the result of intense practice extended for a minimum of 10 years" (p. 363). Ten years is a long time. If you read the article itself (and you should), you will see that Ericsson gets even more specific, stating that true expertise requires an approximate average of 10,000 hours of deliberate practice. When you compare experts to amateurs in any field, Ericsson finds, the difference is the amount of time spent engaging in deliberate practice (Ericsson & Pool, 2016).

You probably do not want to get a PhD in statistics, teach statistics in graduate courses, and write articles on statistical methodologies. Therefore, you do not need to study quantitative research and statistics for 10 years. But Ericsson colleagues' (1993) research is relevant to you because it clearly demonstrates that getting better requires this kind of effortful, attentive engagement that they call *deliberate practice.* In fact, it is the *only* way to get better. Reading this book (assuming you are giving it your full attention) is an example of deliberate practice. Conducting your own quantitative research studies is another example. With engagement and time, you will get better. Asking for your engagement and time is asking a lot, however, which brings us to the importance of motivation.

Motivation. One thing I appreciate about Ericsson's (Ericsson et al., 1993; Ericsson & Pool, 2016) work is the way it highlights the devotion required to be good at anything. It places talent on a spectrum. If you have a hobby, perhaps you devote a few hundred hours of deliberate practice to art or golf or piano. If you want to be an expert, the demands are much greater. If becoming an expert simply means lots of hours of deliberate practice, why are there not more experts?

Ericsson and colleagues (1993) answer this question when they wrote, "The most cited condition [for optimal learning and improvement] concerns the subjects' motivation to attend to the task and exert effort to improve their performance" (p. 367). Put simply, motivation is critical. Who can stomach deliberate practice of anything for any considerable length of time if there is not some intrinsic motivation? Motivation should not be taken lightly. Student affairs is not a high-paying career. You must be motivated to pursue student affairs, and our field loses more than half its professionals in the first five years (Renn & Hodges, 2007; Tull, 2006). The job is hard enough even without seeking to become a scholar practitioner. Are you reading this book because you have to or because you are motivated to learn something useful to make yourself a better student affairs professional? You do not learn statistics by accident. You must have the motivation to put forth the effort required for learning, and once you have the motivation, you need to find good teachers.

Mentorship. The last of the Five Ms is mentorship. By mentorship, I mean good teaching. Good teaching is hard to find, and the quality of teaching partly determines the extent to which a person learns and uses quantitative research and statistics. A primary reason I am writing this book is to provide guidance and teaching that does not currently exist. There are books on statistics that go much more in depth than this one, but part of good teaching is meeting students where they are to help them take the next step in their learning.

This book presumes you know little about quantitative research and statistics and that you care about student affairs. There are not too many books that fit those parameters. I am honored to be your teacher, and I hope you have other teachers in this area either now or farther along your journey.

During my own education, I was amazed at how little I could learn in a research or statistics course and still make good grades in the course. I shoved concepts into my short-term memory, spit them back out appropriately, and rarely understood how to apply them. I encountered my first good statistics teacher in my doctoral program. Laurie Schreiner, my statistics mentor, explained statistics conceptually, and she did not focus on mathematical formulas. All her examples were from higher education, and she found ways to keep me engaged through difficult material. She laid a foundation for me, and I wanted to learn more. But I had no one else to teach me. So I started reading books on statistics, forcing myself to read every word whether I understood it or not. I took notes along the way, trying to put concepts into my own words. When I finished one book, I would pick up another book from another author who covered the same material. Something about the way multiple authors discuss concepts in slightly different ways penetrated my thick skull. Things started to make sense. Synapses and myelination were forming. I was learning.

This is not how I recommend you learn quantitative research and statistics. In fact, I write this book to help you avoid having to learn that way. If you do not have access to a good teacher in person, in Chapter 12 I recommend some good books that I used as sources for this text. But whether in person or on paper, you need mentors who can guide you along the way.

So there you have it: The Five Ms for learning quantitative research and statistics: mind-set, myelin, mastery, motivation, and mentorship. To learn quantitative research and statistics as a student affairs professional, you must believe in your capacity to learn, grow, and change. You must insulate those synapses in your brain, making those connections faster and stronger. You must spend time in deliberate practice and find the internal motivation to work hard at learning. And you must find people who are a few steps ahead of you and who are good at explaining these concepts.

What Accountability Is Supposed to Do

Higher education is in the golden age of accountability (although few would use the adjective *golden* to describe it). The importance of higher education can still be demonstrated through many life outcomes. Nevertheless, skepticism grows among the public, the government, and the media regarding the state of higher education in the United States.

In an age of accountability, numbers matter. For the foreseeable future, quantitative research will remain important in accountability conversations. Tuition outpaces the cost of inflation, and just about everyone wants colleges and universities to justify their costs.

Meanwhile, the amount and proportion of money institutions spend on administrators is growing in comparison to faculty (Hacker & Dreifus, 2010). Faculty do not like this, as you can imagine. When budgets need to be tightened or even reduced, faculty will continue to demand cutting administrators. And what administrators will be perceived as the easiest to cut? The ones who are all about fun and games, of course! If student affairs professionals desire to survive budget cuts, they must demonstrate that they offer students much more than entertainment. Student affairs professionals are vital to the educational experience of college students, but they must demonstrate this fact. If student affairs professionals desire to demonstrate how they contribute to retention, engagement, achievement, and learning, they will need to do so through quantitative research and statistics (Sriram, 2017).

Accountability is quickly becoming a derogatory word in higher education. No one in higher education should be surprised that stakeholders are concerned about costs and want to know that money is well spent. Accountability is supposed to prevent those in higher education from becoming lazy, from going through the motions and not paying close attention to learning and related outcomes. Higher education should be held accountable, and administrators should take the lead in making sure colleges are meeting goals. Instead, accountability becomes about meeting minimum requirements to satisfy those holding the stick (or the carrot). This leads to boring work. The curiosity and passion for improving the lives of college students is quickly sucked away. Is higher education missing the point of accountability? Perhaps so, which is why I recommend that you stop doing assessment altogether.

Stop Assessing and Start Researching

I am calling for the end of the use of the term *assessment* by student affairs professionals (Sriram, 2017). I used to think that assessment was a good thing; it was a catchall for the kinds of evaluative endeavors student affairs professionals embarked on. Research, by contrast, was a higher, more magical endeavor conducted by faculty. When I reflected on this difference, it did not stand up to even slight scrutiny. Why would an activity be called assessment if done by a professional but called research if the same activity was conducted by a professor?

I then thought maybe the difference between assessment and research was not about who did the activity; the difference was in the activity itself. This is what I now commonly hear. Assessment is about evaluation, whereas research is about discovery. But this notion does not stand up to scrutiny either. When you evaluate, are you not making a discovery? When researchers evaluate the effects of state funding on higher education, would that not be *just* assessment? These scholars call it research, however, and they publish it in the top journals. The idea that assessment is evaluation, and research is more ambiguous or theoretical is difficult to defend. Some research is practical and directly informative; some is more theoretical without immediate, direct implications. All research is drawn from theory but not always to the same extent. Different research endeavors serve different purposes, but this is no reason to call some of it research and some of it something else (Sriram, 2017). If you are trying to discover truth based on other people's search for truth, you are conducting research. I cannot imagine any assessment project worth doing in which you are not trying to discover truth. I cannot imagine any assessment project that does not draw from theory and inform theory. Therefore, I think it is time to do away with the term *assessment* altogether.

Let's stop assessing and start researching. This does not mean all research is created equal. There is a spectrum of quality and rigor with research. You should not necessarily think that one side of the spectrum is better than the other; it is simply more rigorous. Rigor is often good, but it is sometimes unnecessary as well. You do not need every research endeavor to be the most rigorous possible. You may want some research to be generalizable across the nation or beyond. You may want some research to be generalizable to only a subpopulation on a single campus. The scope of what you want to know should determine the scope and rigor of your research. But less rigor or a smaller scope does not make it something other than research. Figure 3.1 illustrates how research can be placed on a spectrum, from small-scale to large-scale research.

Fried (2002) suggests that student affairs professionals engage in action research, which is becoming popular in settings such as K–12 education. Action research is research on a smaller scale, similar to assessment. Likewise, Malaney (2002) refers to himself as an *applied researcher* in student affairs, another term for someone who does action research. My question is, Why do we need these terms? Action research, applied research, assessment—they all do more harm than good. Let's do research, and as we conduct our research, let's discuss the rigor, scope, merit, our hopes and dreams, the truth we discovered, and most important of all, what it can mean for others (Sriram, 2017). Let's do student affairs work with a research paradigm.

My goal for the Introduction and the first three chapters of this book is to lay a foundation for what you are doing and why you are doing it when it comes to research in student affairs. In the next chapters, I want to discuss how to do it. It is time to get our hands dirty.

Figure 3.1. The research spectrum.

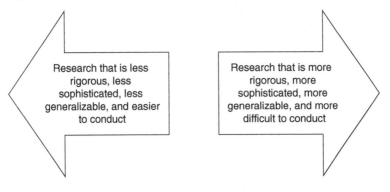

Review Questions From This Chapter

Use the following review questions to test yourself. When you test yourself, you force yourself to recall information, and the act of recalling leads to better and deeper learning.

- What does it mean to have a research paradigm?
- How can a research paradigm lead to more challenging and more meaningful work?
- What is a growth mind-set, and why is it important?
- What can research on talent and expertise mean for you as you try to learn quantitative research methods and statistics?
- What is the difference between assessment and research? (Careful—this is a trick question.)

4

RESEARCH DESIGN

Erin was excited about the research project she conducted on her campus concerning underrepresented students. She felt as if students of color were not experiencing the same level of a sense of belonging as White students on her predominantly White campus. Her intuition and experience (student affairs fast) told her there was a difference between the two groups of students, and now she was ready to search for truth on this issue (even if it might mean her intuition was wrong). She formed a committee, led the development of a new survey, administered the survey, and received more responses than she expected. But her enthusiasm quickly vanished when she began to analyze the data. She realized in hindsight that she should have asked other survey questions than the ones she asked. She also began to doubt whether the information she gathered would answer the questions she really wanted answered. Erin invested much time and energy into this research, and now she wished she could go back in time and do it all over again.

The Importance of Planning and Design

Stephen Covey (2004) famously advocated to begin with the end in mind. Planning is difficult for a number of reasons. It takes a lot of energy and returns little satisfaction. Planning also seems to get in the way of actually doing the kind of work you want to do. Thinking is hard. So instead of doing a lot of hard thinking early, why not just do a little bit of thinking at various times along the way? Putting off the hard thinking is a trap all too easy to fall into.

With research, planning on the front end is crucial to prevent frustration and fruitless efforts. The work that research requires is worth it only if you discover the truth about what you specifically want to know. You may have heard of Murphy's law, which is often paraphrased as "Whatever can go wrong will go wrong." As popular as that saying is, it does not reflect what people actually think. Instead, people err in the other direction. Humans tend to be victims of optimism bias, or the belief that whatever can go right, will go right (Kahneman, 2011). People go into projects naively thinking that most, if not everything, will go as it should. For this reason, humans are horrible at meeting deadlines or budgets, even when they themselves get to set the deadline or projected budget.

Research requires a constant shifting between the big picture and the small details. It is all too easy to get so caught up in the small details that you forget the question you are trying to answer. I always make sure to keep a few key notes on a single page in front of me when working on a research project. One of the items on this page is my research question (or questions), and I am amazed how often I need to read it. I find myself drifting off track while trying to keep all the details of the research project straight. Reading basic information about my own research study gives me my bearings, like a compass. For any research project, you must know what type of research design you will use and what exactly your research question is. I want to give you limited options to both of those needs (research design and research question) to avoid unhelpful complexity and help you learn.

Two and a Half Research Designs You Need to Know

Quantitative research has basically two ways to approach a research endeavor. I say *basically* because there are certainly more nuanced options, but these two represent the major choices. These two choices come down to one question: Are you conducting an experiment in which you sort your participants into groups or not? When you can place your participants into groups of your choosing, you are conducting an *experimental research design*. When you do not, you are conducting a *nonexperimental design*.

Experimental Research Design

Experimental designs are traditionally considered the gold standard of research designs. New, highly sophisticated statistical methods are getting to the point where they can imitate experimental designs, but I tend to agree with tradition that experimental designs are still the gold standard. Here's why: In an experiment, you choose in which group to place your participants. Another way to state this is that you can choose the *treatment* (program, policy, or some other type of intervention) any participant gets. To better understand this, I give you two examples, one from medicine and one from student affairs.

Let's pretend you have a new medicine you believe will cure the common cold. You are pretty excited about this new medicine and the potential for it to cure the world of an annoyance. How do you discover the truth about whether this medicine works? One way is to give people who have a cold this medicine and see if they get better. But if you think critically about this approach, it has several flaws. Everyone who has a cold gets better (eventually), so how can you know that the medicine works simply from people getting better? The best way to learn the effects of your cold medicine is to have a comparison group. If you could recruit 200 people who have a cold, and you gave 100 of them a sugar pill and the other 100 your new medicine, you could then compare how long each group takes to get over the cold. This is a better design, but there are still flaws. One flaw is that not all people have the same immune system. People differ in their amounts of sleep and exercise (both of which are important for overall health and resiliency). You have 200 people in your study. How do you account for all the little differences among these 200 people? In other words, how do you make sure your two groups are as equal as possible? You can try to make the groups equal on one or two variables by placing people into groups manually, but this gets extremely tedious when you start to analyze even a handful of variables (e.g., sleep, exercise, gender, age, etc.). So what do you do?

The answer is randomization. Beautiful, wonderful randomization. Randomization, the hallmark of experimental designs, is randomly assigning each participant to one of your groups. The magic of randomization is that it randomizes every variable you are thinking about and every variable you are not thinking about. So while you are thinking about sleep and exercise in your study, you are also randomizing for hair color, height, and favorite candy. When you randomize, you ensure that your groups are fairly equal on everything. When you now compare your randomized groups, you can make cleaner, more effective comparisons between the sugar pill and your new cold medicine. If you want to discover more truth, you can design three comparison groups: one that takes a sugar pill, one that takes a cold medicine currently on the market, and one that takes your new medicine. With this slightly more complex design, you can determine how your new medicine compares to doing nothing and how it compares to a medicine that is already available.

Experimental designs can be similarly helpful in student affairs work. Let's say you are the director of orientation programs in your division of student affairs. As part of orientation, you take students to an off-campus retreat center for the day. There is a debate among your staff concerning which retreat center to use. There are two retreat centers within driving distance, and your staff strongly disagree on which one is better. In fact, they are pretty passionate about the debate. Rather than go with the more persuasive argument, you decide to engage in student affairs slow by turning this into an experiment. You ask your vice president if you can take half of your students to one retreat center and the other half to the other one. You tell her that although this will create more work for all of you this one year, it will allow you to discover which retreat center students like more. She agrees, and you develop a survey to measure students' feelings about the retreat center. (I will teach you how to develop such a survey in the next chapters of this book.) To make better comparisons, your department randomly assigns students to one retreat center or the other. With randomization, you have confidence that the two groups will be fairly equal on gender, race, in-state or out-of-state status, and other factors that could be important but that you have not even thought about yet. When you compare the two groups on satisfaction, you can better attribute the results to the particular retreat center. Voilà! An experimental design.

Nonexperimental Research Design

The moral of this story is that you should always do experiments (if only life was that easy). The idea of sorting participants randomly into groups of your choosing is simple to understand and difficult to do, especially in higher education. Random assignment can often lead to ethical issues or logistical nightmares. For example, if administrators of a college want to determine if the campus recreation center makes a difference for students, they could give only half of the students—randomly selected—access to the recreation center and then compare the two groups on health or satisfaction. But how do you ethically tell the other half of the students they cannot have access to something that other students can access? Or perhaps you desire to compare whether one residence hall provides a better experience for students than another residence hall. There is nothing unethical about randomly assigning students to one hall or the other. But unless your college has a tradition of random room assignments, you are likely to encounter significant backlash from parents and students for not taking their rooming preferences into account.

These types of practical problems lead those in higher education to often conduct nonexperimental research studies. Nonexperimental designs have other names, such as *survey research* or *correlational research*. *Nonexperimental* is a limiting term because it is describing what the research is not rather than what the research is. I still prefer the term, however, because it directly connects to the key question I mentioned earlier: Are you conducting an experiment or not? In nonexperimental research design, you use numbers to describe trends, attitudes, relationships, or opinions of a group (Creswell, 2014). You are not sorting participants into different groups of your choosing, but you still might compare groups that are already present.

Let's take the two examples I used earlier and modify them to fit a nonexperimental research design. The first example had to do with your new medicine to cure the common cold.

How do you discover the truth about whether this medicine works if you cannot sort people into groups and have one group take your new medicine? This is a significant limitation, but all is not lost. Let's say you somehow got approval to put your medicine on the market. You could then survey a large number of people and ask them questions about how often they get a cold, what medicines they take to deal with the cold, and how long it takes them to get over their cold. You could also ask questions about how they feel about their cold medicine. Once you have these data, you can use statistics to identify patterns among the different medicines and see if some medicines seem to fare better than others. Cause and effect becomes much more difficult to determine in this research design, but you can still determine statistical significance and effect size (discussed in Chapter 7). In other words, you still get valuable information that helps you to discover truth. The information is not as clean as in an experimental design. But sometimes you just cannot do an experiment. Also, sometimes doing a nonexperimental design allows you to examine many more people (for instance, if there was already an existing database that has information on people's colds and cold medicines).

Quasi-Experimental Research Design

In my previous student affairs example, you were curious about which retreat center might be better for your orientation program. Let's pretend that you cannot randomly assign students to one retreat center or the other. Instead, perhaps you have two groups of students on two different dates, and you receive permission to send one group to one retreat center and one group to the other. You cannot mix the two groups because of the different dates. But you can still survey all the students about their orientation experience and their perceptions of the retreat center. Once you have this information, you can then look for patterns and make comparisons. You can still use the retreat center as a variable and see how it relates to measures of satisfaction. You are still comparing the two retreat centers, but the students you compare were not randomly assigned to those groups. Therefore, this type of design is a *quasi-experimental design*. Quasi-experimental designs are set up similarly to experiments, but the groups occur naturally and without random assignment.

In the title for this section, "Two and a Half Research Designs You Need to Know," the two and a half designs are experimental, nonexperimental, and quasi-experimental (the half design). Experimental designs compare groups into which people are sorted based on random assignment, thereby equalizing the groups on all variables. Nonexperimental designs do not compare groups, per se, but rather identify relationships among variables in the data. Quasi-experimental designs compare groups that preexist, not only

Figure 4.1. Two and a half research designs.

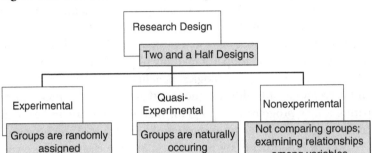

allowing you to make comparisons but also letting other variables possibly get in the way of the truth you want to discover. Figure 4.1 displays these designs. All three designs are valid, important, and helpful. However, I want to make a case for conducting more experimental designs in higher education.

It's Time to Experiment

Experimental designs dominate research in fields such as medicine and psychology. If you search the literature in the field of higher education, however, you will have a difficult time finding a published study using an experimental design. Why? I already mentioned that experiments can be more difficult and can involve ethical and logistical challenges. All three of those issues (difficulty, ethics, and logistics) are valid, but I want to address how you can overcome them.

Difficulty. Experimental designs require a lot of planning from the outset. You need to be able to manipulate your groups and randomly assign participants before anything else happens. You must be proactive. Other approaches allow you to be a bit more reactive, with you making these decisions after you collect data. As much work goes into the before part of an experiment as it does in the after. Sometimes this means giving one group a treatment, whether it is a program or policy or physical environment, and doing nothing with the comparison group. Other times, to make even better comparisons, you can create an experience for the comparison group so that it mimics the treatment group in every way possible except for that one variable you want to compare. For example, medical researchers have learned it is better to compare a group that takes a sugar pill to a group that takes a new medicine. It would be easier to have the comparison group not take any pill at all, but the very act of taking a pill can have psychological benefits that can improve health and perceptions of health. In student affairs, this might mean comparing a new program to a program that already exists rather than comparing a new program to the complete absence of any program.

So yes, experiments are more work, but the clearer picture you get of cause and effect, and the ability to create fairly equal groups on every variable imaginable, is worth the effort. The beauty of experiments is that they are simple to understand and powerful in terms of the design and statistics. You can explain an experiment to someone who knows nothing about quantitative research and statistics, and your audience will understand the value and the conclusions. Explaining nonexperimental designs is more difficult without also explaining how statistics work. The direct comparisons of experiments are more comprehendible than the relationships among variables in nonexperiments. Experiments are pure and powerful.

Ethics. If experimental designs are worth the difficulty, then what about the ethical issues involved with giving one set of students a treatment (that you think will benefit them) and designating another set of students as a comparison group (without the benefit)? In other words, how can you ethically do something to students that is harmful? Well, you cannot ethically harm students. But I think professionals are sometimes too quick to conclude that conducting an experiment poses an ethical dilemma. If you know that one treatment (whether it is a program, policy, environment, or experience) is better than another, then there is no reason for you to conduct the experiment in the first place. You conduct the experiment because you do *not* know, and the experiment will help you to discover truth on the matter. As an example, you might believe that a living-learning program is better for students than a traditional residence hall. The purpose of the experiment is to put this belief to the test (student affairs slow) so that you can find out if your hunch (student affairs fast) is indeed correct. As a professional, you must always do what is best for students. Experiments help you to determine what is best, and there is nothing unethical with putting your best guesses to the test. Once you have evidence that one experience is truly better than another, you are then ethically obligated to try to bring that experience to as many students as possible.

Logistics. Logistically, experiments can feel daunting. The question of how you randomly sort people into anything without causing conflict is a fair question to ask. It helps to try to think in terms of randomly assigning the treatment to people rather than randomly assigning people to the treatment. Let me explain that further. Random assignment is one of the fairest ways to make decisions. It removes all bias. This does not mean, however, that you must declare to your students that they were randomly assigned to anything. One of the problems with research on living-learning programs is what scholars refer to as *self-selection.* Making comparisons between students who are in living-learning programs and those who are not is problematic because students who choose living-learning programs may be different in a number of ways from other students. (I have encountered this problem in my published research.) When students self-select into a treatment, whether a program or residential environment, they exhibit a certain amount of internal motivation that might heavily influence any effect you find from the treatment.

What would really be wonderful is if someone randomly assigned students to different residence halls and then compared the results. This kind of comparison would provide a clearer picture of the truth regarding the effect that different residential environments have on students. You can randomly assign the residence hall to the student because you do not yet know what difference any residential community has on students. You can then make some powerful comparisons. If students complain about their living situation, you can still move them to another residential community, but you should then exclude those particular students (because you have moved them out of their random assignment) when you make comparisons between the two groups in your statistical analyses.

Experiments do require extra effort, consideration of ethical issues, and a willingness to handle more logistics. The extra effort is worth it, and we need more experiments in higher education. Ayres (2007) notes that businesses are relying on experiments now more than ever to determine the best strategies with their customers.

Rather than business leaders only arguing about what they think is the best approach, they increasingly use experiments to let the customers' voices be heard. The same can and should apply to student affairs practice. Rather than only relying on the opinions of professionals in staff meetings (student affairs fast), we should also let the students' voices be heard through experiments (student affairs slow). But whether you conduct a research study with an experimental, nonexperimental, or quasi-experimental design, the key to your research is the question you seek to answer.

Four Categories of Research Questions

The point of a research design is to help you discover truth regarding a question. Without good questions, you cannot find good answers. The thought of there being infinite questions available to you can be daunting. If you then try to match a research design and statistical method to each of those infinite questions, statistics becomes daunting also. You need categories to help you. Fortunately, researchers discovered that there are—essentially—only four categories of questions you can ask in quantitative research and statistics. Four is not so daunting, is it? When I discovered there were four types of research questions, it changed everything for me. I finally had a scaffold for building my statistical knowledge. The information I learned no longer felt like random facts I was trying to desperately hold together. I offer four categories of research questions, based on the work of Tabachnick and Fidell (2007): relationship among variables, comparing groups, predicting groups, and analyzing structure (see Figure 4.2). With each of the four categories, I provide an example of a possible research question for that category.

Relationship Among Variables

Example research question: To what extent does participation in multicultural programming, membership in student organizations, or classification of year (first-year versus returning student) influence a sense of belonging in African American students?

In nonexperimental designs, you search for the extent to which certain variables relate to one another. In fact, examining the

Figure 4.2. Categories of research questions.

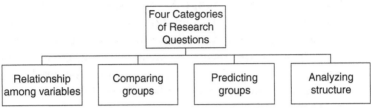

relationship among variables is the most popular type of quantitative research question. The beauty of this type of question is that you can ask it *after* you have collected data. Or perhaps you discover that data have been collected by other people for other purposes, and you can now use that data to ask your own questions. For example, if your institution participates in national surveys of students, you may be able to get access to the raw data (data that have not been analyzed or manipulated) of those surveys. You can then analyze how some variables relate to engagement, satisfaction, or anything else that surveys might measure. Within this research question category, you make judgments of how variables relate to each other, but you must be careful to not falsely assume that one variable causes another variable simply because the two variables relate to each other. As statisticians like to say, correlation does not prove causation.

Comparing Groups

Example research question: To what extent does a sense of belonging differ among African American students, Latina/Latino students, Asian American students, and White students?

Research questions regarding the comparison of groups use experimental or quasi-experimental designs. As a reminder, random assignment to groups makes the design experimental, whereas comparing groups that occur naturally is quasi-experimental. When you compare groups, you search for any significant differences among the groups on one or more variables. You might compare male students to female students. Or you could compare students in one residence hall to students in another. Or, if conducting a true experiment, you might randomly assign students to one program versus another and then compare the two groups. As you might imagine, questions regarding the significance of group differences are frequently used in higher education and student affairs research but much more frequently with quasi-experiments (naturally occurring groups) than true experiments (randomly assigned groups). In this example of a research question, you cannot randomly assign students to a particular race. Therefore, this question uses a quasi-experimental research design.

Predicting Groups

Example research question: Can first-year African American student persistence to the second year be predicted from participation in multicultural programming, membership in student organizations, or GPA?

Predicting group membership is a type of research question that is not used as frequently but can be powerful in certain contexts. When students fall into one of two groups or categories, you can analyze data in hindsight to predict which group they should fall into based on any number of variables. As illustrated in the example research question, one of the most common uses of this type of question is retention. After students complete their first year at your institution, they fall into one of two groups. They either persist or leave your institution. You can go back and analyze variables such as first-semester GPA, major, high school GPA, entrance test scores, and socioeconomic status (just to name a few) to determine to what extent those variables predict whether a student persisted. Because you already know which students persisted and which ones did not, statistical software can develop a formula for predicting groups that is the most accurate possible with the variables you choose. You can then use this formula to predict which first-year students will persist or not persist in future years, allowing you to consider how to help those students who are predicted to not persist.

Analyzing Structure

Example research question: Is there construct validity in a psychometric instrument designed to measure the sense of belonging of college students?

This type of question concerns itself with analyzing the underlying structure of a set of variables. In other words, this type of question searches for patterns on how variables fit together. A common use of this category of question is to validate surveys. Methods used with this type include factor analysis, principal components analysis, and structural equation modeling. When survey designers claim that "these five items measure engagement" or "these six items measure student-faculty interaction," they base those claims on analyses of structure.

In subsequent chapters, we will go through specific statistical methods used under each of these types of question. But before we really get going with statistics, I want to spend a couple of chapters teaching you how to develop surveys.

Review Questions From This Chapter

Use the following review questions to test yourself. When you test yourself, you force yourself to recall information, and the act of recalling leads to better and deeper learning.

- What are the two and a half research designs you should know?
- Which research design is better, and why?
- What are the four types of research questions for quantitative research?

5

THE THEORY BEHIND
SURVEY DESIGN

Jeff is trying to figure out how to help increase the interaction students in his residential community have with faculty. This semester, he started a program called Two Sides. Jeff chooses a particular topic and invites two faculty members to engage students in a conversation on the topic. The perspectives of the two faculty members purposefully differ to encourage critical thinking in students. Jeff hopes this program will not only help students learn to think in more complicated ways but also improve the perceived approachability of faculty. He makes sure to have lots of great food at the events, tries to keep the events from going too long, and purposefully leaves time at the end so that students and faculty can talk informally.

The housing department is conducting an end-of-the-semester survey of students, and Jeff has the opportunity to add questions. He is interested in a quasi-experimental design, comparing the attitudes toward faculty of students in his residential community to students in other residential communities without Two Sides or a comparable program. He knows his research question will be one on comparing groups, but comparing groups on what? In other words, how can he measure students' attitudes toward faculty so he can compare students in his residential community to other students?

The Importance of Surveys in Student Affairs

Sometimes research in student affairs uses measured variables such as GPA or categorical variables such as retention. More often than not, however, the variables of interest to student affairs professionals pertain to perceptions, attitudes, and opinions. To measure these types of variables, researchers use surveys. Surveys are dominant in student affairs, but knowledge of how to properly create them and use them in data analysis is not as dominant. Malaney (2002) laments this fact.

> I believe that methodological standards of survey design and administration in higher education in general, and student affairs specifically, have been relaxed severely over the past few decades to the point now where many individuals are practicing survey research without a clue as to proper methodology. (pp. 139–140)

Malaney has a point. I agree that few in student affairs know how to properly design surveys. But I also believe that anyone can learn how to do it, and I think you can start doing it after reading this chapter and the next one. That is not to say, however, that you will be an expert after reading two chapters of this book. You will get better through practice over the coming years. So on the one hand, I do not want student affairs professionals to continue to create and administer surveys when they do not know what they are doing. But on the other hand, I want to take survey design off some mysterious pedestal and help student affairs professionals begin to learn these needed skills now.

Some Important Background Information on Surveys

We did not always have surveys as a measurement tool. The development of surveys has a history. According to DeVellis (2017), Isaac Newton was the first person credited with using the average of multiple observations as a way of taking an overall measurement. Newton did this in the 1670s. About 100 years later, Daniel Bernoulli examined the distributions of values (how scores spread and cluster together) and noted that any measurement is going to have some amount of error. In the late 1800s, Charles Darwin's work on evolution and his observation of variation across species led to the formation of some more formal statistical methods. Sir Francis Galton, who was Darwin's cousin, took Darwin's systematic observation of variation and applied it to humans. A colleague of Galton's, Karl Pearson, discovered the mathematical tools to systematically examine the relationships among variables. Pearson is sometimes referred to as the founder of statistics (DeVellis, 2017).

In the early 1900s, Charles Spearman developed factor analysis, a statistical method that falls under the analyzing structure category of research questions and is important for survey development. At about the same time, Alfred Binet, who was convinced that intelligence is not fixed and can and should be developed in children, created tests to measure mental ability in France (DeVellis, 2017). From there, scholars continued to build on the work of others to make advancements in how surveys and statistics can be used to measure and make sense of phenomena. When the computer was invented, these laborious formulas and calculations began to become increasingly accessible and less time consuming.

Much of statistics, surveys, and quantitative research in general is based on the notion that to have valid research, we must have good ways to measure things. But what is measurement? Measurement is when you assign numbers to identify different degrees of a quality of some event or object. When you assign numbers to try to represent good or bad or large or small, you are measuring. Psychometrics is a subspecialty that is concerned with the measurement of psychological and social phenomena. You can get a PhD in psychometrics, so the depth and sophistication goes well beyond what I will teach you in this book. Nonetheless, I want to teach you to become a budding psychometrician.

Before getting into the how-to of surveys, it is important to understand them from a theoretical perspective. A theory is a way of explaining things, a way of thinking about something. There are different theories (or ways of thinking) about surveys. The theory I use in this book is the classical measurement model, which is also referred to as *classical test theory*. This theory is the most common one for survey development, but it is by no means the only one. In fact, some would argue that it is not the best theory. I stick with classical test theory because it is well established and easier to understand and use than other theories. Please keep in mind that any theory will have its advantages and disadvantages.

Understanding the Latent Variable

The most important concept when developing surveys is the latent variable. Every survey starts with your desire to know something, the search for truth. What you want to know, what you want to measure, is your latent variable. A variable is something that can be observed or measured and that varies in amount or quality. The term *latent* means hidden. Many of the variables of interest to you in your work in student affairs are not directly observable (measureable). Examples include beliefs, motivational states, emotions, attitudes, and perceptions. By contrast, a GPA is directly measurable. The number of times a student participates in a program is also measurable. But what if you want to measure student satisfaction? You cannot walk up to students, take out a tape measure, and measure their satisfaction. If you wanted to know students' height, by contrast, you could do just that. You could even argue with the students about their height because you have an objective measurement. You cannot argue with those same students about their satisfaction. Yet, you are still trying to measure their satisfaction, albeit indirectly. Height is a variable, but it is not a latent variable because it is not hidden. Satisfaction, which is more hidden, more subjective, and hazier, is a latent variable. Other examples of latent variables you might be interested in include sense of belonging, attitudes about diversity, perceptions of learning, engagement or involvement, mental health, academic confidence, and aspects of maturity. By no means is this an exhaustive list; I list these possibilities to trigger some latent variables you could be curious about.

Once you understand the concept of a latent variable, you need to understand the idea of a *true score*. This is a bit weird, but stick with me. Because the variable is latent, you cannot ever know the actual level, or score, of the variable. If you are interested in student satisfaction regarding a program of yours, satisfaction becomes your latent variable. You must first admit that you can never objectively know the exact level of satisfaction in your students. This exact level is referred to as the true score. You cannot enter students' minds and find out the true score. So the true score is a way to talk about the goal of perfect measurement, even though perfect measurement is not possible. Although perfect measurement is not possible, imperfect (or indirect) measurement can be extremely useful. Herein lies your hope. You cannot directly measure student satisfaction regarding your program. But you can measure it indirectly and try to get close to the true score.

This is where classical test theory comes into play. Classical test theory states that if you attempt to indirectly measure a latent variable multiple times, you can estimate how close you are to getting to the true score. This is great news. You want to know about student satisfaction (your latent variable). You want to know the true score, but you also admit that you cannot know the true score. Mathematically, you can put a measurement of your latent variable on a scale from 0 to 1, where 0 is horribly inaccurate and 1 is a perfect measurement. Therefore, the number 1 represents the true score. This is a mathematical trick. You cannot know the true score, but you can still give the true score a value of 1, which represents a perfect measurement.

At this point, I want you to understand that a latent variable is the hidden, psychological variable you want to measure. The true score is the actual amount of that latent variable in the people you want to measure. Classical test theory is a theory of survey development that uses multiple, indirect attempts at measuring a latent variable to get close to measuring the true score. With this understanding, I want to tell you more about surveys and survey items.

Understanding Surveys, Scales, and Items

Survey is a general term. It refers to every questionnaire that attempts to gather information from people. When I discuss surveys in this book, I am specifically referring to scales. Whereas a survey is an attempt to collect any information, a scale is a type of survey that attempts to measure something. The way it measures something (i.e., your latent variable) is by asking respondents to use numbers to identify various degrees of a quality.

Let me give you a personal example. When my wife, Amanda, was pregnant with our first child, I was interested in how she was feeling throughout the day. Like any good spouse, I would at random times ask her how she was feeling. She would respond with words like *okay* and *fine*. It did not take me long to realize this was getting me nowhere. I was collecting information through my own oral, one-question survey. But the responses were not giving me the information I needed. I was not measuring. After I realized I was dissatisfied with my survey, I made a slight modification. Instead of asking, How are you feeling? I began saying, Please put how you are feeling on a scale from 1 to 100. Most spouses might think this is crazy, but this is the sort of thing my wife puts up with constantly. So without protest, she started providing me numbers on a scale when I would ask. In my first survey question, I never knew the difference between okay and fine. But when I started getting numbers like 72 and 81, I could easily make comparisons and observe whether she was feeling better or worse since the last time I asked.

When I shared this example with a graduate student of mine, she started using this as an icebreaker with students. She had often started meetings by asking student leaders how they were doing. She started asking them instead to state how they were doing on a scale from 1 to 100. She felt the numerical responses led to much more interesting follow-up conversations because she had a better sense of how her students were doing.

Do you see how my first question (How are you feeling?) was gathering information, but my second question (on a scale from 1 to 100?) was measuring? The only difference was that I was now assigning numbers to represent different degrees of a quality (in this example, the quality of how my pregnant wife was feeling). Collecting information was good, but measuring was great. Surveys collect information. Scales measure. A scale is a measurement instrument composed of multiple questions or items. I use the term *item* because scales often technically use statements instead of questions.

Returning to my example of wanting to know (measure) how my pregnant wife feels, I need to create items for my scale. So instead of asking my pregnant wife one question and asking her to rate it on a scale from 1 to 100, I might use several items, such as the following:

- I feel pretty good right now.
- Right now, I feel as good or better than I did when I was not pregnant.
- I can go about my day right now without thinking about how badly I feel.

I can then have her agree or disagree with these statements and put her responses on a scale. Assuming she does not punch me in the nose for asking her to do this throughout the day, this scale would give me an even better understanding of how my pregnant wife feels. You will learn more about how to create scale items in the next chapter. For now, I want you to know that classical test theory uses multiple items to indirectly measure your latent variable.

The Likert Scale

Whenever you seek to measure a latent variable, you must provide your respondent with a format for responding. There are numerous response formats, and DeVellis (2017) is a great source to explore different variations. I refrain from discussing all the options here because I think I will better serve you by writing about the one I think is most useful for your work. When I initially gave my wife my one-question scale, I gave her a range from 1 to 100. For my new, three-item scale, I have changed the response format. The three items (e.g., "I feel pretty good right now") require her to agree or disagree with each one. A simple agreement or disagreement could work, but that format fails to capture the intensity of the agreement or disagreement. So my scale has two important parts. The first part is the *stem*—a statement expressing an opinion. The second part is the *response option*—a series of descriptors indicating the strength of agreement with the stem. This popular scale is referred to as the Likert scale, named for the University of Michigan professor who created it.

I need to give my wife choices for her response that go beyond simply agreeing or disagreeing with each statement. The number of choices I recommend (and have had the most success with) is six. Why six? Because people can easily grasp the idea of high, medium, and low. So, essentially, you are asking your respondent to agree or disagree with each statement and to do so on a high level, medium level, or low level. Specifically, the response options would be listed like this: 1 = *strongly disagree*, 2 = *moderately disagree*, 3 = *slightly disagree*, 4 = *slightly agree*, 5 = *moderately agree*, and 6 = *strongly agree*. Notice there is no true middle response option. You could create a seven-item scale that has a neutral option (*neither agree nor disagree*), but I have never found that to be helpful. Also, respondents will tend toward the neutral answer if you provide it, which is even less helpful. Therefore, I prefer forced choice scales, which are even numbered and do not provide a neutral response option. I discuss the Likert scale in more detail in the next chapter. For now, I want to stay theoretical, and the next theoretical concept I want you to be comfortable with is validity.

Validity

One of the harder concepts to grasp with surveys is validity. This is for good reason, as validity is a little complicated and messy. Even as I try to define it, I find myself needing two definitions. The first definition of *validity* pertains to whether you are measuring the variable you are trying to measure as opposed to accidentally measuring something else. The second definition pertains to whether you are reaching the appropriate conclusions based on your findings. Porter (2011) published a great article on college student surveys and validity that I highly recommend. He discusses how validity is the degree to which evidence and theory support the scholar's interpretation of the survey results. To help you grasp the multifaceted nature of validity, I focus on four aspects of validity, each beginning with the letter C: content validity, criterion-related validity, construct validity, and conclusion validity.

Content Validity

Content validity is a facet of validity that focuses on whether items measure what they are supposed to measure. Let me give you a personal example of how content validity works. As I get older, I notice that I might also be gaining weight. So I decide to buy a bathroom scale to measure my weight. This scale is valid as long as it actually measures my weight. The scale is valid as long as I use it only to measure weight. If one day I wake up feeling badly, worried that I might be getting sick, and jump on my scale to measure my temperature, the scale is no longer valid. It is still measuring weight, even though I am now interested in body temperature. Nothing changed about the scale to make it invalid. What made it invalid was how I used it: my own need for content that was not reflected by the scale. This is content validity.

Content validity may make sense when thinking about a bathroom scale versus a thermometer, but it gets less clear when dealing with latent variables. How do I know if my scale that I hope measures satisfaction actually measures satisfaction? Looking at the content is not the only way to determine validity, but it is a good first step. Questions to consider when designing a scale are, How were items created? Where did the items come from? What is the justification for including these items? The answers should directly and indirectly lead back to the published literature on the subject. (Remember: Research is the search for truth based on *other people's* search for truth.) For content *validity*, the concept should be well defined, and the content of the scale should reflect the conceptual definition and the previous research and findings on the concept.

Another step for ensuring content validity is to have a group of experts review your scale's items. You should define *expert* in a way that makes the most sense for you and your purposes. If I were creating a scale to give to students on my campus, I would want the input of those student affairs professionals on my campus who have an interest and experience in the latent variable my scale measures. If I were trying to validate the scale on a national level, I would want people whom I consider national experts on the topic to review my scale.

Criterion-Related Validity

Criterion-related validity (also known as *concurrent validity*) is based on comparison. One way I can check to see if my bathroom scale is valid is to compare it to the results I get when I step onto other bathroom scales that I believe to be valid. Likewise, one way I can check the validity of my survey scale is to compare it to a similar scale that I am confident is valid. For my student satisfaction scale, I am going to review the literature to educate me on the best items to create for the scale. Perhaps when reviewing the literature, I come across another student satisfaction scale that someone else created and published. Maybe there is information on the validity of this scale in the article, and other scholars also use this particular scale. In this case, I am fairly confident that the scale is a valid measure of student satisfaction. I could just use this same scale for my own purposes (giving proper credit, of course). But if the scale covers the same general topic but does not quite capture the information I want to know, I could instead include some of these criterion scale items and compare those responses to the responses of the items that I create myself. If people respond to my scale items in ways similar to the criterion scale items, I have evidence that my scale is valid. As you may have already noted, this is more of a practical approach to validity than a scientific one. But it is a helpful approach to validity nonetheless.

Construct Validity

A more sophisticated and statistical form of validity, construct validity concerns itself with the relationship of a variable to other variables. Remember that a variable is anything that you can measure and that varies. So in one sense, college student satisfaction is a variable. But in another sense, each and every item I use in my instrument (scale) to measure college student satisfaction is also a variable. You can think of variables as having levels or layers. College student satisfaction is a variable that could have all sorts of subvariables (e.g., satisfaction with classes, satisfaction with the living environment, satisfaction with student organizations, satisfaction with student affairs programs). If you pick one of those subvariables, such as satisfaction with student affairs programs, you can then develop items to measure college student satisfaction with student affairs programs. If you create five items for your scale, these five items represent another level of subvariables. So now we have three levels of variables: Level 1 (college student satisfaction), Level 2 (satisfaction with student affairs programs), and Level 3 (five items used to measure satisfaction with student affairs programs). Figure 5.1 displays this idea visually.

Thinking about levels of variables can seem complex, but I only share this with you to help you understand there are various ways

Figure 5.1. Levels of variables.

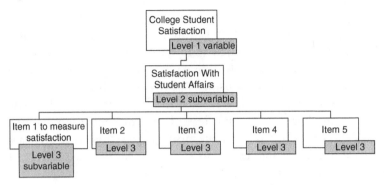

to think about variables and their construct. The good news is that there are no right or wrong answers. Rather, construct validity concerns itself with the choices you must make as a scholar practitioner about your variables and your ability to use statistical evidence to defend that your choices are valid. You can also use this evidence to refine and improve your choices.

Of our four types of research questions, construct validity deals with the research question category of analyzing structure. Here, you search for the underlying structure to variables by using statistical software to determine whether your items relate to one another and therefore measure the same latent variable (or construct). So after I create my five items to measure student satisfaction for my student affairs program, I will use the instrument to gather information from as many students as possible. I can then input these data into the statistical software, and the software will tell me to what extent my five variables relate to each other. If all five of them highly relate to each other, I can presume (based on classical test theory) that they are indirect measurements of the same latent variable (student satisfaction with my student affairs program). If four of them highly relate, and one of them does not, I can assume that the fifth item is an invalid measurement of this latent variable and remove it from my scale. If none of them highly relate to one another, then I can probably assume that my scale does not have construct validity. This would be unfortunate news, but it would also be truth. Truth is never completely unfortunate news.

Conclusion Validity

So far, you have learned that content validity deals with whether the scale measures what it is supposed to measure. You also learned that criterion-related validity is comparing your scale to another scale that is already deemed to be valid. Next, you learned that construct validity is using statistics to analyze the structure of variables to determine how well the items of your scale relate to one another. Last but not least, I present conclusion validity, the extent to which the conclusions you draw from your scale are logical and justifiable based on the information you gathered. I hope some examples will show how easy it is to make mistakes with conclusion validity and how important it is to not make such mistakes.

Let's say you start a new student affairs program. To your delight, more students participated than you expected, and most of them responded to your satisfaction survey. When you created the instrument, you made sure to draw from the published litera-ture and to ask for feedback from experts to ensure content validity. You found another measure of student satisfaction in the litera-ture and included those items in your scale. This let you establish criterion-related validity. You then conducted a principal compo-nents analysis (you will learn about this later) to help you analyze the structure of your items. As a result, you found that your scale had construct validity. You are thrilled that your scale is valid. Addition-ally, students reported high levels of satisfaction with your program, which is more good news. You run to your computer and e-mail your vice president of student affairs to tell her that students want more programs like this one. You also tell her that you have evidence to support your claim.

Did you happen to catch the mistake you just made (hypotheti-cally)? Where did you go wrong? Well, you did not measure whether students want more programs like yours; therefore, you cannot claim that students want more programs like yours. You measured student satisfaction with your program. The only valid claim you can make based on your evidence is that students were indeed satis-fied with your program. Any other claim you make is not valid (in the sense that it is not supported by the evidence you gathered). You can certainly make the argument that you should put on more programs like this one because student satisfaction with the program was so high, but you need to be clear that such an argument is your opinion, not the opinion of students. This might seem like a subtle difference, but it is a rather important one.

People make mistakes with conclusion validity frequently. A common example of this mistake is with college entrance tests such as the SAT or ACT. Have you ever heard people make claims about the intelligence of students based on these scores? That is an invalid claim. The SAT and ACT are aptitude tests—they test specific content areas. They are not intelligence tests, and they do not claim to be. Yes, these tests are somewhat predictive of college performance (which adds to their criterion-related validity), but the only claims that can be validly made on these tests is that some students did better on these specific content areas than other students. That may be helpful information, but it is separate from claims of intelligence. For a claim to have conclusion validity, the claim must be based on the evidence collected. Figure 5.2 displays the Four Cs of validity.

Prioritizing the Four Cs

Validity is complicated and a bit messy, but it is not beyond your ability to understand it. If you are a beginner with developing surveys, trying to tackle all four of these Cs could be overwhelming. I certainly do not want to scare you off by teaching you about validity. Instead, I want to encourage you to take steps in caring about the validity of your surveys and your claims about the results of your surveys. To this end, I recommend you begin with content validity and conclusion validity. Of the Four Cs, these two are the most practical and the least statistically oriented. Yes, I want you to

Figure 5.2. The Four Cs of validity.

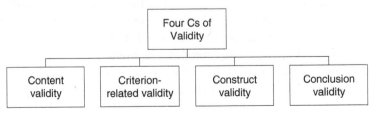

eventually feel comfortable with all of the Four Cs, but two is better than zero for now.

Content validity requires you to dive into the research on your topic, which is an important step to take anyway. Reviewing the literature will help you develop better survey items that cover the whole content area. Reviewing the literature will also form you into more of an expert on the topic. Speaking of experts, I like the accountability of having people you trust serve as experts on your items. Let them review your items and provide feedback on the content and the clarity of the items. Ask these experts for item suggestions you have not included. You are not obligated to incorporate all the feedback you receive, but it will make you aware of blind spots. Personally, I have created some really bad items that I had no idea were bad until others pointed it out. As soon as they gave me the feedback, it was like a blindfold had been lifted from my eyes. I completely agreed with their feedback and saw the items in a whole new light.

Conclusion validity, on the other hand, keeps you focused on the point of your research, which is the question you are trying to answer (and also the questions you are not able to answer through your research). Finally getting results from research is a great feeling, and you will be tempted to celebrate by making all sorts of wild and unfounded claims about what your results mean for the universe. Take a deep breath, remain objective, and ask yourself what your results do and do not mean.

Start with content validity and conclusion validity. I rarely find criterion-related validity useful because if you can find a scale in the literature that measures what you are trying to measure, then why not just use that scale? Why are you developing your own scale and reinventing the wheel? Typically, I am creating my own scale because something like it does not exist in the literature (and therefore I do not have a criterion with which to compare my scale). I do find construct validity very useful, but it requires familiarity with statistical approaches such as factor analysis. I want you to get to that level of familiarity eventually, but I do not want you to feel like you must master those approaches before you can do anything meaningful about the validity of your scale. The counterpart to validity is reliability. Fortunately, reliability is an easier concept to discuss.

Reliability

Reliability is the accuracy of your measurement. To go back to my previous example, if I want to know my weight and I step onto my bathroom scale, I have a valid measurement because my bathroom scale will actually show me my weight. But reliability pertains to how well it shows me my weight. The bathroom scale I purchased claimed to be accurate to 0.2 pounds. Less expensive scales might be accurate within 0.5 pounds. A more expensive scale might be accurate to 0.1 pounds. These differences in accuracy represent differences in reliability.

A thermometer is another good illustration of reliability. If you take your temperature multiple times in a row, rarely do you get the exact same reading. Did your temperature really change in those five seconds? Probably not. Thermometers are not perfectly accurate. But good thermometers will get close to giving you the same reading because they are more accurate. A reliable instrument will perform in more consistent and predictable ways. So although validity deals with whether you are measuring what you intend to measure, reliability is how well you measure it.

Another way of thinking about reliability is how well a scale gets to the true score of a latent variable. As I mentioned earlier, the true score is the actual, unobservable level of a latent variable. You can never know the true score, but mathematically you can think of the true score as perfect and give it a value of 1 (measuring accuracy on a scale from 0 to 1). Classical test theory states that even though you cannot know the true score of a latent variable, you can at least determine how well the responses to the scale items of your latent variable relate to each other (DeVellis, 2017). If they highly relate to each other, you can presume that they measure the same latent variable. How well they relate to each other can be an indication of the scale's reliability.

There are multiple ways to think about reliability. One way is test-retest reliability, which is comparing back-to-back results (tests) to see how similar they are to each other. If you take multiple measurements in a time span in which you do not expect the latent variable to change, you can then see how closely the measurements are to one another. For example, when I take my temperature multiple times within one minute, or when I step on my bathroom scale several times in a row (that can't really be how much I weigh!), I am gauging the test-retest reliability. I could gauge the test-retest reliability of my scale by giving it to the same group of students twice within a short time span such as a week to see if their responses are similar.

Another way to think of reliability is internal consistency, how well items in a scale relate to each other. The typical measure of internal consistency is Cronbach's alpha, which takes the response scores of all items in a scale and determines how well those items relate to each other. This relationship is put on a measurement scale from 0 to 1. Remember that the true score is assigned a value of 1. Cronbach's alpha results in a number between 0 and 1, which is the reliability (statistical software will compute the Cronbach's alpha for you). Therefore, the true score (1) minus the reliability (Cronbach's alpha between 0 and 1) equals the *error* of the measurement. For example, if your satisfaction scale produces a Cronbach's alpha of 0.81, you now know three things: the reliability (0.81), the true score (always 1), and the error (1 − 0.81 = 0.19). This brings up the question: What is a good enough Cronbach's alpha for a scale to be deemed reliable? This is not a black-and-white question, but I am going to give you a black-and-white answer: 0.70. I think that a Cronbach's alpha of 0.70 is acceptable, 0.80 is good, and 0.90 is great.

I have covered a lot in this chapter on surveys. Even in trying to share only the vital information, it can still be overwhelming. I want you to know what is in this chapter, so please reread if necessary so that you can properly use surveys for your work in student affairs. The next chapter will be less theoretical and more practical as I take you step-by-step in how to develop a good scale.

Review Questions From This Chapter

Use the following review questions to test yourself. When you test yourself, you force yourself to recall information, and the act of recalling leads to better and deeper learning.

- What is measurement?
- What is a latent variable?

- What is a true score?
- What is a scale?
- What is validity?
- What are the Four Cs of validity?
- What is reliability?

6

SURVEY DESIGN
IN PRACTICE

L amar had mixed feelings after reading the chapter on the theory of survey design. Part of him felt inspired. He loved the call to be a scholar practitioner. He felt motivated by the idea of becoming more of an expert, respected for his knowledge and his ability to learn and adapt. And he knew that surveys are an important tool for student affairs slow. Learning about latent variables, classical test theory, scales, validity, and reliability certainly stretched his current knowledge. But he also felt pessimistic. Beginning to grasp some of these concepts was affirming, but he still felt a long way from actually creating a valid and reliable survey. Lamar is ready to go from theory to practice.

Steps to Scale Development

You now have a foundation for understanding surveys perhaps as never before. Let's build on that foundation. This book is about equipping you to do student affairs slow in addition to student affairs fast. By being fast and slow you will better serve college students. One of the most important tools in your quest to do student affairs slow is a survey instrument. When done well, surveys provide vital information and allow you to measure things that perhaps you did not know you could measure. I wrote the previous chapter to help you to understand surveys, scales, items, classical test theory, validity, and reliability. In this chapter, I want you to create a scale and put it to use.

When developing a scale, follow these steps:

1. Decide what you want to measure.
2. Create items to measure it.
3. Determine how you will measure it.
4. Develop a plan for validity.
5. Add instructions and pilot test it.
6. Improve it.
7. Administer it.
8. Check for reliability.
9. Improve it again.
10. Do something meaningful with your responses.

The rest of this chapter takes you through these steps. Please note that this book does not explain how to complete the institutional review board (IRB) application on your campus. An IRB is a team of scholars who help to ensure that research does not intentionally or unintentionally harm other people. All research endeavors that could possibly be used for presentation or publication should go through an IRB. If you are not conducting research on minors (under 18) and if your scale does not relate to sensitive issues, the IRB process can be fairly quick. But you should certainly give yourself time to go through this process. The benefit of IRB applications is that they force you to do work you should be doing anyway (e.g., developing a rationale for why your research is worth doing, spending time reading the literature, creating an informed consent form).

I use my own example to illustrate each of the steps for scale development. In addition to following my example, I want you to simultaneously create your own example by creating your own scale. You can do this, and it starts with deciding what you want to measure.

Decide What You Want to Measure

The most critical decision for developing your scale is deciding what you want to measure. In other words, what is the latent variable you will try to measure? Remember that a latent variable is a hidden variable usually representing an opinion, belief, or attitude. In every area of student affairs, there is something you want to know. What do you want to know that you do not know already? Because I have spent time as the faculty head of a residential college, I want to know how students feel about faculty support, and I am using this as my example for scale development. I could have said that I want to know how students feel about me in the faculty-in-residence role, but I am more interested in how my role might influence overall student feelings regarding faculty.

Once you have a latent variable, you should label it and define it. Labels are important because they separate one thing from another. I certainly could have called my latent variable *faculty care* or another similar name. I chose *faculty support* simply because I liked it the most from among the labels that came to mind. If you like the name of your latent variable less and less the further you get into the process, you should feel free to change it. Definitions are important because people can use the same words to mean different things. What matters is what you mean by the words you use, and it is vital for you to clearly tell others what you mean. As you move through the steps for developing a scale, you may feel the need to refine your definition. You should feel free to do so. My initial definition of *faculty support* is the extent to which students feel cared for by faculty. This definition could use some elaboration, but I will let my survey items do the elaboration for me. Before you move on to Step 2 and item creation, please take a moment and write down the latent variable you want to measure and a definition of it.

Create Items to Measure It

As I discuss in the previous chapter, you cannot directly measure a latent variable. Therefore, you must measure it indirectly. The main idea behind classical test theory is that multiple, indirect measurements of a latent variable—if the measurements highly relate to one another—can serve as a very good approximation of the true score of the latent variable. These multiple, indirect measurements are your survey items.

Items are the same as survey questions. As a reminder, we use the term *item* because often items are not technically questions. Instead, you provide your respondents with statements they agree or disagree with to varying degrees. Item creation can feel daunting. You do not have a PhD in psychometrics, you may not have a PhD in anything, and you probably hesitate to describe yourself as an expert in anything. To let such thoughts (if you have them) stop you would be terrible, not just for you but for the students you serve (remember that you need a growth mind-set). It would be like refusing to learn how to sew because you could never create designer clothing. Sewing can still be useful to you, even if you will not make your own clothes some day. The way you learn to sew is to study the techniques and practice. There is no magic sewing gene floating around in some people's DNA. Likewise, there is no magic survey gene floating around in the DNA of psychometricians. People get good at survey development by studying the techniques and by practicing. The more you do this, the better you will get. There may come a point where you have no need for or interest in getting better. I want you to get to the point where you are taking good steps based on a foundational understanding of how survey development works. I want you to get to the point where you can use surveys to improve the work you do for students while also avoiding common big mistakes.

So let's begin. You now have a latent variable. You want to create a scale that measures this latent variable based on classical test theory. The next step is to create a large pool of items as candidates for possible final inclusion in your scale. It's like a job interview, and you are the hiring agent. In the first round, you simply review applications. If someone applies, you read the person's application with no filter or judgment. The equivalent of this first round in scale development is to create items as you would in a brainstorming session. Critique is not welcome at this point. You want to create items people can agree with or disagree with to varying degrees. Reading the literature on the topic of your latent variable is a helpful and mandatory precursor to item generation, but let's just go from the gut for now. I want you to try to create five statements related to your latent variable that others can agree or disagree with. The items can capture an aspect or piece of your latent variable, or they can try to target the whole idea. My example latent variable is faculty support. The following are the five items I created out of thin air, simply from my gut and my experience:

1. I feel that professors support me in my educational goals.
2. I feel that professors care about me.
3. I feel that professors want me to succeed in college.
4. I feel that professors want me to succeed in life.
5. I feel that professors are approachable.

I hope you are as underwhelmed by these items as I am. See, I am just as bad at this as you are! However, in reality, there is no bad or good at this point. You are creating the best items you can create in the moment. You may have been surprised by my use of the first person (beginning each statement with I). I have grown fond of this approach because it puts you and the respondent on the same side. If I were to rephrase it in the second person (e.g., "You feel that professors support you in your educational goals") it can come across as accusatory. First-person usage also makes it clear that the student should not respond for other students. The student should only share what he or she believes. I could have removed the introductory "I feel that" for every item (e.g., "Professors support me in my educational goals"). Removing that phrase makes the items shorter and to the point, which is good. But I fear it might be too short and get to the point too fast. As you can see, I am relying a lot on my feelings and intuition (student affairs fast) about items at this stage. Student affairs slow for these items follows soon.

I also did not include any items that measure behaviors. All the items measure feelings, perceptions, and attitudes. If you try to measure behaviors, you are asking for trouble. Porter (2011) does a great job discussing the problems with this behavioral measurement approach. The bottom line is that human beings in general (and college students specifically) are horrible at accurately reporting the frequency of behaviors. If you ask them to report on behaviors, they will do so with great confidence. But their responses will not necessarily be factual. Therefore, you should avoid using items that try to capture frequency (e.g., often, seldom, never). If tracking these behaviors is truly important to what you want to know, you should pick a small group and have the group members keep daily diaries that keep track of such information. Diaries are a wonderful and underused tool for avoiding the pitfalls of poor memories. Instead, I use items to measure attitudes, and I find that attitudes are often more important to me than behaviors. What usually matters are the feelings of the respondents. As the saying goes, perception is reality.

You might have several questions about my example items, such as, Why did you use *professors* instead of *faculty*? I thought that students would know what a professor is, but they may not know what I mean by faculty. I could also define what I mean in the instructions I give before they take the instrument. (Detailed instructions are helpful, and Porter [2011] points out that instructions are an overlooked part of survey development.) Another question might be, How did you know what subtopics to include, such as educational goals, care, and success? I did not know what subtopics to include. I guessed. Some might ask, How do you know if your items are any good? I do not know. Honestly, I do not care. (Okay, I care a little bit, but I am trying not to be judgmental at this point in the process.) Someone else may say, You ask if professors are approachable. How do you know that approachability fits under the latent variable of faculty support? How do you know that faculty approachability is not a latent variable separate from faculty support? That is a really great question and demonstrates how much you have learned so far. Good for you! Again, I do not know if approachability truly fits under faculty support or if it is a separate latent variable. There is a way I can test this down the road, however. (See the section on exploratory factor analysis in Chapter 11.)

A blog post by Seth Godin (2016) argues that the key to improvement is testing. Anyone can write a software program or cook a dish, Godin states. What separates the experts from the amateurs is the process of testing, receiving feedback, making improvements, and testing again. This idea absolutely applies to scale development. Anyone can create good items. Anyone can create bad items. What separates the experts from the rest is that the experts know how to test their scale and improve it.

Please try to create five items (statements with which people can agree or disagree) that relate to your latent variable.

Initially, you should write down the items that come to mind without judgment. But there is a difference between good and bad items, and a few tips will help you create better items. First, items should be clear; this is more difficult than it seems. Often you write items from your perspective rather than from the perspective of your respondent. For my own example scale, using the word *faculty* is a perfect example. When I hear the word *faculty*, I know exactly what it means. To think that students interpret the word *faculty* with the same ease that I do is a costly mistake. Your items should be clear and to the point. They should not be shorter or longer than needed to communicate your statement. Simple words are better than complex words if the simple ones still communicate your point accurately.

Second, you should avoid double-barreled items, which actually ask two things. For example, the item "Professors care about me and want me to succeed" is not a good item. What if respondents feel that professors care for them, but they do not necessarily feel that professors want them to succeed? This item asks the respondent to combine two ideas that are not the same. When you catch yourself with a double-barreled item, simply break the item into two.

Third, use reverse-scoring items cautiously; in fact, avoid them whenever possible. Reverse-scoring items are stated in the negative rather than the positive and require you to flip the response scores before you conduct any statistical analysis. If I had the item, "My professors do not support me," strongly agreeing would now be a bad thing instead of a good thing (contrary to my other items). So if I converted every *strongly agree* response to the numerical value of six (because there are six choices and I want higher scores to indicate stronger feelings of support), I would need to reverse this particular item so that *strongly agree* equals one and *strongly disagree* now equals six. Again, I recommend simply not having reverse-scored items.

Fourth, try to use strong language with your items. If your items are too soft, it will be easy for respondents to choose the extreme ends of your scale. You want variability. You want to try and push your respondents toward the middle so that only those respondents who truly feel extreme about your latent variable respond with extreme scores. Let's take a look at my five items again.

1. I feel that professors support me in my educational goals.
2. I feel that professors care about me.
3. I feel that professors want me to succeed in college.
4. I feel that professors want me to succeed in life.
5. I feel that professors are approachable.

Adding a word here or there, as illustrated in the following list, can make the items stronger and prompt more respondents to use the middle choices (i.e., *slightly agree* or *slightly disagree*).

1. I feel that professors *really* support me in my educational goals.
2. I feel that professors *always* care about me.
3. I feel that professors *absolutely* want me to succeed in college.
4. I feel that professors *really* want me to succeed in life.
5. I feel that professors are *easily* approachable.

It's not Shakespeare, but adding these adverbs can be helpful in getting a more accurate measurement of faculty support.

Fifth, generate as many items as possible. DeVellis (2017) states that there are two primary ways to improve the reliability (accuracy) of your scale. One is to have better items, the other is to have more items. It is important for you to explore as many items as possible for your scale. Redundancy or overlapping items is a good thing. You do not want to wear out your respondents by asking them the exact same question repeatedly, but asking similar questions can serve to double-check their responses. When there is a job opening you are in charge of helping to fill, you do not want only three fantastic candidates to apply. You want 50 candidates to apply so that you can narrow it down to three fantastic candidates for final consideration. The same is true for your scale. The final version of your scale should be somewhere between three to seven items. (This is my way of being helpful by being specific; the true best length depends on your specific needs.) If the final version will be three to seven items, I think you should start with 15 to 20 items. DeVellis (2017) is more extreme: he recommends having an item pool three to four times larger than the number you want for your final scale. The point is the same: Create many more items than you think you will need at the start so you can pick the best items at the end. The more items you have to choose from, the higher the likelihood of your ending with great items.

These five tips (clarity, avoiding double-barreled items, avoiding reverse-scored items, using strongly worded items, and having lots of items) will help you immensely as you practice the art of item creation. When you have a draft of items you believe meet these criteria (to the best of your ability), it is time to determine how to format your measurement. Before proceeding to Step 3, please create five more items for an initial total of 10 items for your scale.

Determine How You Will Measure It

In the previous chapter, I discussed choosing a response format and recommended the six-point Likert-type scale for several reasons. Likert scales are commonly used and therefore are recognizable by respondents and other scholars. Using six response options is a nice balance between a variety of score options and making each option meaningful. You want your measurement to capture variability. More response options tend to capture more variability. But people can only handle so many choices before they feel annoyed or overwhelmed. The six response options I use are *strongly disagree, moderately disagree, slightly disagree, slightly agree, moderately agree,* and *strongly agree*. I use adverbs to be clear about what each item means. If I were to just use *agree* instead of *moderately agree* as the fifth option, respondents could become confused about whether agree means a lot or a little. The word moderately clarifies that I mean in the middle in quality or amount. If I did not want to do a forced-choice response format, I would add a neutral option. That would create a seven-point Likert scale by adding *neither agree nor disagree* in the middle. I do not like neutral options, but it may serve a purpose in what you try to measure.

Measurement is the assignment of numbers to indicate varying degrees of something. For me it is intuitive that a higher level of agreement always corresponds to a higher number. Therefore, 1 = *strongly disagree*, 2 = *moderately disagree*, 3 = *slightly disagree*, 4 = *slightly agree*, 5 = *moderately agree*, and 6 = *strongly agree*. These numbers are what matter because they allow mathematical calculations. You do not need to show your respondents the corresponding numbers, however. You can simply have your respondents circle or click on the response of their choice and then you translate those responses into numbers when you enter the data in a spreadsheet or in a statistical software program.

If you want to explore other response formats, DeVellis (2017) is a good place to start. For now, please add these six options (*strongly disagree, moderately disagree, slightly disagree, slightly agree, moderately agree,* and *strongly agree*) as response choices beneath each of the 10 items in your scale.

Develop a Plan for Validity

Look at you! You have a scale! Now it is time to validate it. In the previous chapter, I discussed my Four Cs of validity: content validity, criterion-related validity, construct validity, and conclusion validity. I also suggested that content validity and conclusion validity are good places to start, as these are the more theoretical and less statistical forms of validity. To begin, let's walk through content validity and conclusion validity. I then provide an overview of how you can also put criterion-related validity and construct validity to use.

Content validity. Content validity means much more than whether your scale items look and feel right. The first thing to do with content validity is to connect your items to the literature. Ideally, you would review the literature about your latent variable first, before drafting items. Reading the literature will inform your intuition and improve the items you create. But for the purposes of learning about scale development, I want you to draft items first. (I admit, I really wanted to see your items and I could not wait any longer.) So we will do this slightly backward. Now that you have a draft of a scale, I want you to read one article on your latent variable.

Finding literature these days is much easier than it used to be. This is how I do it (and if I do it, it cannot be too complicated). Open a web browser and go to Google Scholar (https://scholar .google.com), Google's search engine specifically for scholarly works. You can use the power and resources of Google while automatically eliminating works that are not academic in nature (random websites, news stories, etc.). I find Google Scholar helpful and easy to use. To find an article that relates to your latent variable, type in the name of your latent variable and perhaps add the phrase *college student* to increase the likelihood of finding articles that study college students. This part can get tricky because you might use a term that is different from the term used in published research. For example,

I named my latent variable "faculty support." When I type *faculty support college student* into Google Scholar, I get some good articles, but nothing that matches "faculty support." I do get articles that use the more general term *student-faculty interaction*. I could therefore click on those articles or do another Google Scholar search using *student-faculty interaction college student*.

The goal is not to earn your PhD in the topic of your latent variable (at least not yet!). The objective is to find one article that gets fairly close to what you care about. How do you find that one, best article? You should first rely on the titles of published works. Scholars get made fun of for their boring and lengthy titles, but these titles are extremely helpful when you are trying to discern what the article is about without reading it. Find two to three articles with titles that interest you because they seem to connect with your latent variable (even if the authors use a slightly different term for the latent variable). Once you have those articles, read their abstracts (an abstract is a short summary at the beginning of an article). From there, you should choose the one article that you think is worth reading based on the title and abstract. Faculty become experts in a particular topic by learning how to quickly discern what is worth reading and what is not worth reading. No one has the time to read everything. Finding relevant articles is a trick of the scholarly trade. After you make your choice, read the article and highlight the sentences that grab your attention.

If you start to feel that the article is not about what you hoped it was about, read one of the other two articles you selected as finalists. If you really like an article, make sure you use the references at the end as a guide for what to read next. You are letting the author of the publication do the work of finding good and relevant articles for you. Only read as many articles as you want to read. No more. This is for you, your work, and for the benefit of your students. But it is due diligence to at least read one scholarly work to help you with content validity. As you read the article, do you see a connection between your items and the ideas discussed in the article? Do you want to rename your latent variable, or do you like the name you chose? Does the article help you think of additional items you can add to your scale? Please go to Google Scholar and find the best article you can related to your latent variable. Read the article and have the draft of your scale readily available for you to review.

We are not yet done with content validity. You need a panel of experts. Do not be intimidated by the term *expert*. Perhaps *panel of people whose competence you trust* is a better way to describe it. The idea here is that at this point you have spent enough time with your scale that you are now biased. You wrote it, you edited it, you know exactly what everything means. It is time for some external accountability. Who is competent in regard to your latent variable? How much competence do you require? If your scale is national, then look nationally for your panel. I am guessing that your scale is for local purposes (on your own campus). If my guess is correct, then look on your own campus for your panel. With my latent variable of faculty support, student affairs professionals who make efforts in their jobs to connect students and faculty outside the classroom come to mind. I will also see if any faculty members or scholar practitioners on my campus research student-faculty interaction or something similar to faculty support. Another possibility is for me to take my scale to faculty whom I consider to be models of faculty support and ask them what they think of my items.

When you select your panel, I suggest meeting panel members face-to-face, giving them a hard copy of the scale, and asking them to describe their reactions to it immediately after completing it (or even while they are completing it if they prefer). This in-person interaction will allow meaningful conversation. You can immediately ask clarifying questions, and you can even offer changes on the spot and get feedback from your panel member on those changes. If meeting in person is not logistically feasible, send the panel member your scale in an e-mail and ask for her or his overall thoughts on each item. A word of caution: Your panel will most likely not consist of people who are experienced at developing scales. Therefore, some of their advice will be contrary to what you have learned about proper scale development. Do not feel obligated to make the changes suggested. Your goal is to discover suggested changes and then to discern if those suggestions will indeed improve your instrument. For example, you might hear "These items are redundant" when you know that redundancy is a good thing. Do not defend yourself with your panel member (you risk coming across as rude). Take copious notes on everything suggested during your conversations with all panel members. Only after you have collected feedback from everyone can you go back to your office and start making decisions on changes. If you have spent time on the literature regarding your latent variable and also have presented your scale items to people whom you deem competent, you have done a lot to ensure that the content of your scale is valid. You are now ready to think about conclusion validity.

Conclusion validity. When you check for conclusion validity, you ensure you are not getting ahead of yourself with your scale. Conclusion validity is powerful because it connects to big-picture components of your research (e.g., your research design) and detailed components of your research (e.g., the wording of your items). Scales have conclusion validity when the interpretations (conclusions) of the results align with the actual results. So an appropriate, big-picture question to ask yourself once again is, What do I want to know in my research? It is amazing how easy it is to lose sight of what you want to know. When you begin to check for conclusion validity, you should also check your research design, research question, and your research question type (Recall the four categories of research questions from Chapter 4: relationship among variables, comparing groups, predicting groups, and analyzing structure).

Going back to my scale, I want to know how students feel about faculty support. More specifically, I want to know the extent to which students feel supported by faculty, especially outside class. But if you reread the beginning of this chapter, you will see that I want to know more than just that. What I really want to know is if students feel more supported by faculty because they live in my residential college where I serve as a faculty in residence. Answering that question will take more than a good scale; it will also require a good research design. My scale will potentially measure the extent to which students feel supported by faculty. My research design will potentially answer whether living in my residential college has anything to do with those feelings. How will my research design accomplish this task? I need a research design that relates to the research question category of comparing groups. I need to compare students in my residential college with other students. The most apparent choice would be to compare students in my residential college with students in a traditional residence hall on my campus. I would want to pick a residence hall that has a similar composition of students but that does not have the intentional faculty interaction of my residential college.

Because I am not assigning students randomly to the traditional residence hall or my residential college, I am conducting a quasi-experimental design. If there were a way to randomly assign students, I would have a more powerful design and be able to make stronger conclusions regarding cause (faculty interaction in a residence hall) and effect (feelings of faculty support). If I do not randomly assign, I need to adjust the conclusions I make from my results. I can no longer firmly conclude that significantly higher levels of faculty support in students who live in the residential college are because they live in the residential college. That is not a valid conclusion. What I can do is suggest that there is evidence that indicates the residential environment could be a contributing factor in the difference between the two groups. In other words, it is a meaningful claim, but a purposefully softer claim.

On the details level, I need to take a second look at my items. What do my items address? The conclusions I make from my study should directly align with what I am asking in my items. If I am interested in particular subareas of faculty support, I need items that measure those subareas. It would be unfortunate for you to go through the trouble of a research project only to discover a truth you were not originally interested in. By checking, double-checking, and alternating between a bird's-eye view and the ground floor, you will develop a clear sense of what you can and cannot claim as a result of your study. At this time, please write down your research question, your research question type, and your research design. Next, review your items and double-check that the information you desire aligns with what your items measure. When you feel good about your items, it is time to give your instrument a practice run.

Wait. What about criterion-related validity and construct validity? These are important forms of validity, but they both require knowledge of statistics. I provide a foundation for that knowledge later in this book. But I do not want you to give up on creating a scale because you are intimidated by these more sophisticated forms of validity. If you can make a concerted effort with content validity and conclusion validity, you have my permission to move forward. If, however, you want to take it to the next level, then good for you!

Criterion-related validity involves comparing your scale to another scale that is already deemed to be valid. If in the literature you found a scale that measures a similar latent variable, you can certainly add a few of those scale items to your scale. Just be sure to properly cite the author and provide a reference. This form of validity is rarely helpful to me because I either find the scale in the literature and simply use that one, or I do not find the scale in the literature, which is the impetus for creating my own scale. Construct validity uses the research question that deals with analyzing structure. For construct validity, I often use principal components analysis. Structural equation modeling is also used to determine construct validity. Principal components analysis and structural equation modeling fall under the larger umbrella of factor analysis. I discuss both statistical approaches in Chapter 11 to help you understand what they do and why they do it. I also provide resources in Chapter 12 if you want step-by-step instructions on conducting these analyses yourself.

Add Instructions and Pilot Test It

It is one thing to get feedback from a panel of experts, and it is another to get feedback from the people meant to complete your scale. The next step in the process of scale development is to find a group of students (assuming your scale is directed toward students) who are like the ones to whom you will administer the scale in your research. I say *like* because you do not want to pilot test your instrument using the same students your instrument was developed to survey. Doing so could bias their results because they would probably have discussed at length your goals concerning the scale after they participated in the pilot.

I suggest bringing this pilot group together and going through the scale at the same time because it creates your own focus group. Have them complete the scale and provide you with feedback. Students can react to the feedback of others on the spot. A student may timidly suggest a change, and before you know it, the whole group is wholeheartedly agreeing with the suggestion. On the other hand, a student may boldly demand a change, but perhaps no other student agrees with the suggestion. Ask the students to take the scale and provide any and all thoughts. Key questions to ask your pilot group relate to the clarity of the scale; ask them, Did you understand all the items? Were any of the items confusing? You can also time the students to determine how long it takes them to complete the scale. Any scale that takes more than 10 minutes to complete is asking a lot from your respondents, perhaps too much. When I created a survey to measure the competencies of student affairs professionals, it took 15 minutes to complete. My rationale was that full-time professionals who were interested in the topic would be willing to give it that amount of time. But normally, I would not create such a lengthy scale. The time it takes for respondents to take your scale should include the time it takes for them to read your instructions.

Instructions can be surprisingly difficult to write. If they are too lengthy, respondents may skip them altogether. If they are too short, they may not provide the needed information to your respondents. Porter (2011) warns,

> Research indicates that the more time respondents spend trying to recall information, the more accurately they report it. This leads to the recommendation that survey researchers use long introductions to questions as a way to increase recall effort (Tourangeau, Rips, & Rasinski, 2000). Most college student surveys unfortunately take the opposite approach. (p. 59)

Porter's advice is just as much about items as it is about instructions. Clarity and conciseness are important. Thoroughness of information is also important, but conciseness and thoroughness are competing goals. You are the scholar, and you must make judgments regarding what is too long and too short. You want to provide just enough information for your respondents to feel comfortable knowing what to do. For my scale on student affairs competencies (Sriram, 2014a), I wrote the following instructions:

> There are no right or wrong answers to the questions of this survey, just your perspectives. For each of the following statements, indicate whether you strongly disagree, moderately disagree, slightly disagree, slightly agree, moderately agree, or strongly agree. Some items refer to your institution. For questions pertaining to your particular institution, please refer to your current place of work even if you have not been there long.

When I piloted this instrument, I originally did not include the part that defines what I mean by *place of work*. Someone in my pilot group asked, "What am I supposed to do if I have only been at this institution for a couple of months?" This is the kind of helpful comment respondents will make that helps you to catch details you previously missed. You need this kind of help. Please find a pilot group, and ask the group to complete your scale and provide feedback.

Improve It

As DeVellis (2017) notes, "Item evaluation is second perhaps only to item development in its importance" (p. 104). In a sense, item evaluation has a role in almost every one of these 10 steps for scale development. In this step, I want you to once again consider all the knowledge you have learned from the literature, your panel of experts, your pilot group, and yourself. Review your items once again and make another round of revisions as necessary, but do not remove any items unless you deem them egregiously bad. You will soon have a more objective judgment on your items, so be patient about the removal of items for now. When you believe you have a scale that is ready, it is time to administer it.

Administer It

When you administer your scale, you should have two goals in mind. The primary goal is the discovery of truth. You worked hard to get to this point, and it is now time to gather valuable data that will inform your thinking and practice. The secondary goal concerns the continual validation and improvement of the scale itself. Although I encourage you to treat the resulting data as real data, I also encourage you to think of this step in the process as a more robust pilot test. Many psychometricians (those who study the measurement of psychological constructs) firmly believe that you should administer your scale once for validation purposes and then a second time to a completely new sample for the purpose of analyzing results. Although that is certainly a more rigorous way to go about the development of your scale (and that rigor would further ensure its validity), I think it is fine to use the same round of data for both purposes. In either approach, the emphasis is the same: Developing a scale properly is not worth the time and effort unless the scale measures something you are interested in knowing about for the long term. You should develop a scale that you want to use over and over again with different samples of students year in and year out. This kind of longitudinal research allows you to not only refine your instrument but also make comparisons and discern any changes in your results over time.

Administering surveys on paper is becoming increasingly rare. It requires the cost of printing and necessitates gathering all your respondents in a place where they can complete the instrument. On rare occasion, this may make sense. For example, if you have a captive audience, such as a series of classes where you will be administering the instrument, it might be preferable to use paper copies. However, the advantages of an online distribution are many. Online survey creation software is readily available, and your institution may have a license for one or more online survey platforms. You can then send an e-mail to your sample with a link to your survey. The survey software will often do simple analysis for you and will also allow you to easily download the results into more sophisticated statistical software. The data are always there when you need them, and little time is spent inputting data yourself.

Communication is critical to the administration of your survey. You must think carefully about what you will say in your survey to help potential respondents understand what it is and why it is being sent to them. Always send a test e-mail to yourself (and maybe to a couple of colleagues as well) so that you can catch any errors. The link to the survey should link directly to the informed consent form. Rather than requiring the respondents' signature, I include a statement at the end that reads, "By advancing to the next part of the survey, you agree to participate in this research." The IRB on your campus can provide feedback on your informed consent and instructions for proceeding. When your respondents click on the next screen, they should see your specific survey instructions before seeing the first items of the survey.

There are different methods for trying to encourage a higher response rate, which is the percentage of people who received your survey and actually take the time to respond. If you send your survey to 100 people, and 15 people respond, you have a 15% response rate. You want a high response rate, but expectations are changing for what is considered a high response rate. Students are receiving more and more surveys, leading them to ignore more and more surveys. Low response rates raise concern for how representative the data are and, therefore, how generalizable the results are (Porter and Whitcomb, 2003). So how high a response rate do you need? I cannot answer that question. But there is a more important question that I can get you to think about. The issue is not so much about how many people responded but whether the people who responded are different in significant ways from the people who did not respond. The technical term for when your respondents differ from your nonrespondents is *nonresponse bias.* So the more important question is, Are the people who responded representative of the group as whole?

For example, if the group that receives your survey is 50% women and 50% men, but your respondents are 80% women, then it is likely that your results do not adequately capture the views of men. If this happens to you, all is not lost. But can you see how such a situation directly connects to conclusion validity? You need to make sure that the conclusions you make about your results are honest and transparent. In other words, when you share the results, express your concern that these results do not adequately capture the views of men (and that you want to work harder to increase male participation in your next round of research).

The number of your respondents is critical to be able to conduct statistical analyses. When I guide graduate students through theses and dissertations, this is the part that gives me the most anxiety. I am always confident in students' ability to create a good scale, conduct good research, and write about it clearly. I am less confident about students' ability to get enough responses to do fun analyses. Ideally, you want 300 responses, allowing you to conduct sophisticated analyses such as factor analysis. I know 300 is a lot to ask. If you do not plan to do factor analysis, I think you can get away with 100 responses. But with 100 responses you must assume that a lot goes right statistically (that you get good quality data). With less than 100 responses, you are not giving the statistics much to work with at all.

Incentives are sometimes used to try to boost response rates. For example, a lottery incentive is when you tell your respondents that their names will be included in a random drawing for a prize. Porter and Whitcomb (2003) found that lottery incentives can have a very small positive impact on response rates, but the incentives should not be too small or too large. For their experiment, Porter and Whitcomb found that a $100 gift certificate had a bigger impact than $50 or $200 (again, the impact overall was only a slight increase in the response rate). Methods that are more helpful than incentives include sending second and third reminders and addressing communications with a personalized salutation (Porter & Whitcomb, 2003). You want to give your respondents a deadline, and you want to time your reminders so they are evenly spaced between your first invitation and your final deadline. When you have selected a method for distributing your survey and determined a plan for reminders (and possibly incentives), it is now time to send your survey to your prospective respondents.

Check for Reliability

This is the moment you have been waiting for! The results are in and it is now time to do something with them. The ultimate quality you want in a scale is for items to highly correlate with your latent variable (DeVellis, 2017). Because you cannot directly measure the latent variable (true score), you will instead examine how well items correlate to one another. If item responses highly relate to each other, then classical test theory suggests they measure the same latent variable. The purpose of this book is not to teach you how to use statistical software (but books I list in the final chapter are a great place to go to for such teaching). I do, however, want to explain how to go about determining the reliability of your scale.

To conduct reliability analyses, you either need statistical software or an add-in for Microsoft Excel. There are many choices for statistical software. The one I use is IBM SPSS (Statistical Software for the Social Sciences). I prefer SPSS because it looks like a spreadsheet, it relies on pointing and clicking more than writing computer code (referred to as *syntax*), others have taught me to use it, and my institution supports it. Any statistical software will be able to conduct the types of analyses discussed in this book. In addition, instructions and video tutorials can be found online for almost any statistical software. So please choose the software that makes the most sense for you. My instructions in this chapter are for IBM SPSS.

Once you have your data in SPSS, you will want to make sure you do not need to reverse code any items. As a reminder, the five items of my example scale on faculty support are

1. I feel that professors really support me in my educational goals.
2. I feel that professors always care about me.
3. I feel that professors absolutely want me to succeed in college.
4. I feel that professors really want me to succeed in life.
5. I feel that professors are easily approachable.

None of these items need to be recoded. If I had as an item "I feel that professors do not care about me," a *strongly agree* response would be bad and a *strongly disagree* would be good. This can get confusing, which is why I recommend avoiding reverse-scored items. But I also understand that sometimes you fall in love with an item that is phrased negatively. If any of your items were phrased negatively, you will need to recode the responses. Simply search the Internet for *recode variables in SPSS* for instructions on how to recode responses.

There are many approaches to reliability. The approach you will take is a measurement of internal consistency called Cronbach's coefficient alpha (or Cronbach's alpha, discussed in Chapter 5, p. 72). Using IBM SPSS, on the menu at the top of the screen, click Analyze, then Scale, then Reliability Analysis (see Figure 6.1).

A table will appear. On the left side of the table is a list of all your variables. On the right side of the table is a blank space for you to move the items over that you want analyzed. Move over all the items that are part of your scale. In other words, do not move over variables that are not part of your scale, such as demographic variables. At the bottom of the window, you will see Scale Label. This is where you give your scale a name, such as in my case, Faculty Support Scale (see Figure 6.2).

You now want to click Statistics on the same page, which results in another window (see Figure 6.3) with a lot of options, and this

Figure 6.1. Conducting a reliability analysis in IBM SPSS.

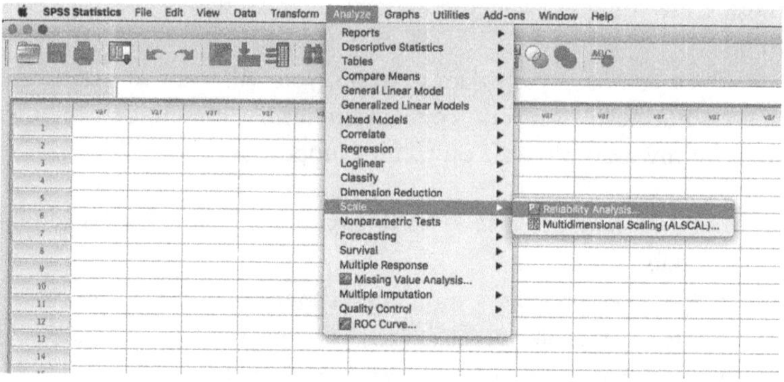

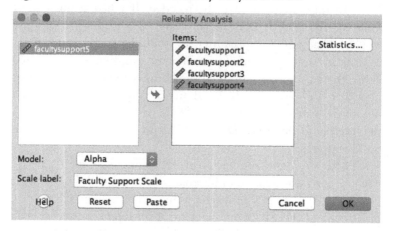

Figure 6.2. Menu options for reliability analysis in SPSS.

can be overwhelming. You only need to select the following three at this point:

1. Item—this will give you statistical information on each item in your scale.
2. Scale—this will give you statistical information on the whole scale.
3. Scale if item deleted—this will tell you what the Cronbach's alpha would be if you were to delete this particular item from the scale.

Figure 6.3. Statistics options for reliability analysis.

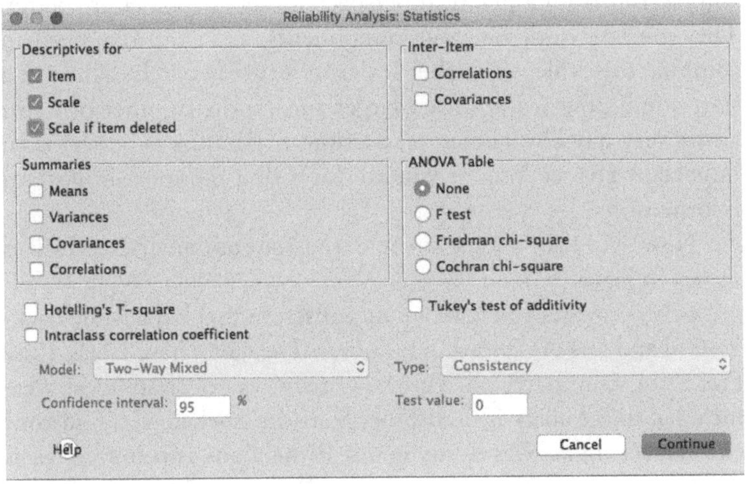

After selecting these three, click "Continue" and then click "OK." Clicking "OK" runs the analysis. Please go ahead and determine the reliability (Cronbach's alpha) of your scale.

Classical test theory states that the internal consistency of your items (how well they relate to each other) is a measure of your latent variable. If the items correlate really well, they are getting close to the true score of the latent variable. Typically, correlations are expressed on a scale from –1.00 (perfectly opposite) to +1.00 (perfectly related). Cronbach's alpha takes every combination of two items and determines how well they correlate. It then averages them. The formula for Cronbach's alpha removes all negative values, resulting in a final number that ranges from 0 to 1.

So what is a good alpha? Here is my rule of thumb, based on DeVellis's (2017) and my own experience:

- alpha = .70 (acceptable reliability)
- alpha = .80 (good reliability)
- alpha = .90 (great reliability)
- alpha = .95 (reliability so great you should consider shortening the scale)

The more items you have in a scale, the more reliable the scale will be. But from a practical perspective, shorter scales are better. They are less work for your respondents, and you may need to combine this scale with other scales in future research. When you start combining scales into a larger survey, the number of items grows very quickly. Therefore, parsimony (simpler is better) is an important goal as long as you are capturing the most important information.

Now, let's take a look at the output of your analysis, which is shown in Figure 6.4.

SPSS provides you with an output screen that has a white background and lots of tables and numbers. The tables have labels. Case Processing Summary tells you how many values (responses) were included in the analysis. Reliability Statistics is where you find your Cronbach's alpha. Was it any good? If the alpha is below .7, all is not lost (mine is .899 in Figure 6.4). The next table is titled Item Statistics where you find the means, standard deviations, and sample sizes for each item (I discuss standard deviation in Chapter 7). The next table, Item-Total Statistics, tells you information about how to possibly improve your scale.

Improve It Again

The far right column of the "Item-Total Statistics" table is titled "Cronbach's Alpha if Item Deleted." This compares each value to your Cronbach's alpha. In other words, it tells you the new Cronbach's alpha if you were to delete that particular item. If deleting the item will make the alpha increase, you should consider removing the item from your scale. This is your objective, measured way of determining what items are good and bad (all in relation to your latent variable). You should delete the item if it will make a big difference in the reliability of your scale. For example, if deleting an item changed the alpha from .75 (acceptable reliability) to .81 (good reliability), I would remove it. If deleting an item changed the alpha from .81 to .82, I would probably think it better to include the item rather than remove it. If my alpha was .96, and deleting an item would reduce it to .91, I might still delete the item to reduce the length of my scale while still maintaining great reliability. With my

Figure 6.4. Reliability analysis of faculty support.

Case Processing Summary

		N	%
Cases	Valid	110	100.0
	Excluded_a	0	.0
	Total	110	100.0

a. Listwise deletion based on all
variables in the procedure.

Reliability Statistics

Cronbach's Alpha	N of items
.899	5

Item Statistics

	Mean	Std. Deviation	N
facultysupport1	3.0909	1.51170	110
facultysupport2	3.9091	1.38501	110
facultysupport3	3.0000	1.42069	110
facultysupport4	3.8182	1.34220	110
facultysupport5	3.0000	1.42069	110

Item-Total Statistics

	Scale Mean if Item Deleted	Scale Variance if Item Deleted	Corrected Item-Total Correlation	Cronbach's Alpha if Item Deleted
facultysupport1	13.7273	21.668	.838	.856
facultysupport2	12.9091	25.038	.634	.901
facultysupport3	13.8182	22.352	.847	.855
facultysupport4	13.0000	25.872	.591	.909
facultysupport5	13.8182	22.352	.847	.855

Scale Statistics

Mean	Variance	Standard Deviation	N of items
16.8182	35.746	5.97883	5

example results, I could consider deleting facultysupport4 because it would increase my alpha and decrease the number of items in my scale.

You will notice that not all items are created equal. Some items will drastically change the reliability if you delete them, whereas others will barely change it. This is an indication of the relative importance (influence) of each item. If you originally developed many more items than you needed (as I suggested), you should now have plenty of items from which to choose. This gives you lots of opportunities to delete items and improve the reliability of your scale. Although numbers are helpful to determine which items you should remove, do not leave out theory. Think through the items and determine if removing an item makes sense to you in regard to what you want to measure. Never let the numbers do all the thinking for you. Just because you are learning to think slow does not mean you should stop thinking fast. Please determine the reliability (Cronbach's alpha) of your scale and make decisions about whether to remove any items.

Do Something Meaningful With Your Responses

At this point, one of two results has occurred. Either you have a scale that is reliable and you are happy about it, or you have a scale that did not reach our .7 cutoff and you are discouraged. Even if you fall into the latter category, I am not discouraged for you. Both situations are learning experiences. If your scale was not reliable, and you could not make it reliable through item removal, ask yourself three questions. First, when you read your items, do they seem to honestly capture the same latent variable, or could they possibly measure different latent variables? Is it possible that your brainstorming and item creation processes went too far off course? Second, did you include enough items? In my example, I only include five items to illustrate what items look like without belaboring the point. But five items are what you want in a final scale, not in the developmental process. I asked you to create 10 items so that I did not wear you out as a beginner. Ideally, and as I mention in Step 2, your scale should have 15 to 20 items so that you have plenty of items to select from in the end. Third, what is the size of your sample? You need enough responses so you have enough data to properly conduct the statistical analyses. I recommend 100 responses as a minimum and 300 as ideal.

But what if you have a reliable scale? Well, you must celebrate! Take friends or family out to dinner (but do not tell them why you are taking them to dinner—nerd alert!). After you celebrate, it is time to get back to work. The purpose of your scale is to measure a latent variable. Measurement is the assignment of numbers to indicate the quality of a value. You can now assign a number to your latent variable by taking the responses of the items in your final scale and adding them. For example, my scale on faculty support is five items, and each response is scored from 1 (*strongly disagree*) to 6 (*strongly agree*). My scale had good reliability with all five items (.899). That means that I can have a final measurement between 5 (if someone responds *strongly disagree* to all five of my items) and 30 (if someone responds *strongly agree* to all five items). The maximum score of your latent variable will depend on how many items are in your final scale. In IBM SPSS or in Excel, you can create a new column that calculates the final score of your latent variable for each of your respondents by adding their responses to all your final items. This is a powerful moment: You are now in a place where you can represent your latent variable by a single number.

Once you have a total score for your latent variable, you can now use it in various statistical analyses. You can use it to ask any of the four types of research questions discussed in Chapter 4: relationship among variables, comparing groups, predicting groups, and analyzing structure. You just took an important step to improve student affairs practice and to improve the experiences of college students. The next step is to learn how to analyze this new variable you have created (and other variables that might relate to it). In other words, it is time to learn statistics.

Review Questions From This Chapter

Use the following review questions to test yourself. When you test yourself, you force yourself to recall information, and the act of recalling leads to better and deeper learning.

- What does it mean for an item to be double barreled?
- What is one way to improve the validity of your scale?

- What is the minimum number of respondents you need to test your scale? What is an ideal number of respondents?
- What is the recommended method for checking reliability called?
- What is the minimum score for a scale to be considered reliable?
- What are the advantages and disadvantages to having more items in a scale?

7

BASIC STATISTICS

S akina was in her office when she noticed an e-mail with the subject "Assessment Report: Action Steps Required." When she opened the e-mail, Sakina saw an attached report with recent survey data from students who had participated in her orientation program. The e-mail asked her to review the results and create an action plan for how she was going to improve orientation based on this feedback. Sakina's report would soon be combined with other similar reports as part of the university's accreditation process. As Sakina reviewed responses to questions, she was puzzled about what to do next. All she saw in the report were averages of the responses to each question in the survey. She wondered, Isn't there more to think about than averages? What do I do with this? What is good? What is bad? Is an average of 3.7 for a specific item something I should brag about? Or should I be worried? Sakina feels frustrated, anxious, and confused. Then, in a moment of revelation, she realizes she can close the e-mail and move on to other ones in her inbox.

Overview

I hate averages. Okay, I do not really hate averages, but taking the average of multiple numbers is as sophisticated as most student affairs professionals get with statistics. There is so much more. You must get beyond the average. I do realize, however, that you are probably not interested in becoming a statistician. So it is my job to teach you what I think all student affairs professionals should know without telling you more than you want or need to know. This book may be the beginning toward your becoming an expert in statistics. Or it may be as far as you go. Either way, I firmly believe that the knowledge from this chapter will help you in your student affairs work. Welcome to Statistics 101. This chapter covers five important concepts regarding statistics: descriptive statistics, inferential statistics, normal distribution, statistical significance, and effect size. Every student affairs professional should be knowledgeable about at least these five concepts. In my own learning, I found that reading chapters on statistics multiple times helped me immensely. Although I will try to teach these concepts as clearly as I can, if you feel as if any of it goes over your head, do not be discouraged. Instead, learn what you can, and commit to reading this chapter multiple times. Each time you read it, something that did not make sense before will suddenly click.

Samples and Populations

As you recall, measurement is the assignment of numbers to represent a quality of a variable. Once you have that assigned number, you have a statistic. So measurement is the process of assigning numbers, whereas statistics are the representative numbers themselves.

When you are working with data, you work with a sample, a population, or both. Your *population* is the entire group that you care about in a particular research project. It is the entire group of people you could collect data from. If you are interested in the sense of belonging in African American college students, then your population consists of all African American college students. If you are interested in the sense of belonging of African American college students who attend your particular college, then your population becomes all African American college students at your college. The population can change depending on the nuances of your research interests. Your population is the answer to the question, What people do you care about in the broadest sense?

Your *sample* is the group of people from whom you actually collect data. My population might be all African American college students on my campus, but my sample is those African American college students who respond to my survey. You want your sample to be representative of your population. If I want to know about African American college students across the nation, I should try to collect data from African American college students at campuses across the nation. If I want to know about the African American students on my campus, and I decide to only send my survey to African American students in student organizations (because I have access to them through my work, for example), my sample is not as representative as it should be. African American students in student organizations may be different from African American students not in student organizations, especially in terms of their sense of belonging. Therefore, I should do one of the following things: (a) figure out how to send my survey to all African American students on my campus or (b) change my population from African American students on my campus to African American students in student organizations on my campus.

Two Types of Statistics

You should think carefully about your population when crafting your sample. This becomes important as you understand the two types of statistics: descriptive statistics and inferential statistics. Descriptive statistics describe your data. Your data are comprised of the information you gathered from your sample. Therefore, descriptive statistics describe your sample. Inferential statistics make inferences from your sample to your population. When you infer something, you make conclusions based on some evidence. In inferential statistics, your evidence is your sample, and the inferences are the conclusions you make about your population based on your sample. You may be familiar with this concept from political election polls. Statisticians take a representative sample of people and ask them whom they will vote for. From that sample, statisticians make inferences to the population (all voters) and are able to conclude with varying accuracy who will win the election. Descriptive statistics describe your sample, and inferential statistics infer things from your sample to your population (see Figure 7.1).

Figure 7.1. Two types of statistics.

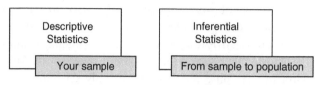

Descriptive Statistics

Once you understand the two types of statistics and their differences, you are ready to go one level deeper. There are four types of descriptive statistics, and each serves a helpful purpose: central tendency, variability, relative position, and relationship. There are multiple calculations that fall under each of these umbrellas. To keep things as simple as possible, I only provide you with one calculation under each umbrella that I think is the most important for you to know.

Central Tendency (Average or Mean)

The good news is that you are already familiar with the first type, central tendency. Central tendency includes those calculations that attempt to capture the typical value of a group. The calculation most used in central tendency is the average (or mean). You grew up using averages in school. Averages are how your grades were calculated. The college GPA is a good example of how averages are commonly used on college campuses.

In the previous chapter, you created a scale to measure your latent variable. Assuming your scale items are reliable, the next step is to take the sum of your response scores to calculate the number that represents the measurement of your latent variable. Therefore, each respondent will have a score for your latent variable. For all respondents, you can then calculate the average of those new latent variable scores to determine the typical score of your latent variable in your sample. In Microsoft Excel, you can calculate the average by using the formula =AVERAGE(FirstCell:LastCell).

Variability (Standard Deviation)

As I mentioned earlier in this chapter, I have a love/hate relationship with averages. It is a useful and common calculation, but it is limited in its usefulness. This limitation can be overcome, but the problem is that everyone knows how to calculate an average, and not enough people know statistics beyond averages. If there was one thing I want you to know about statistics that you might not already know, it is standard deviation. Yes, standard deviation is a slightly more complicated concept, but my goal is for you to know, understand, and use standard deviation from here on out.

Standard deviation is the average distance of scores from the average. Examples will make this fuzzy statement clear. I have two sets of scores in Table 7.1.

As you can see, the two sets are very different from each other. Set A has a wide range of scores, and not a single score shows up twice. Set B has a very small range of scores, with only two unique scores listed in the whole set. The problem is that the average of both sets is 5.5. If average is meant to capture the typical score, it does a good job of that with Set B. It does a horrible job with Set A. There is nothing typical about 5.5 when examining Set A. Therefore, we need another number that will tell us how much the scores vary from one another. This second type of descriptive statistic is variability, and the most popular way to determine variability is standard deviation. Standard deviation tells us how much the scores

TABLE 7.1
Two Sets of Scores

A	B
1	5
2	6
3	5
4	6
5	5
6	6
7	5
8	6
9	5
10	6

vary from the average. The following are the steps for calculating standard deviation:

1. Calculate the average. (The average of Set A in Table 7.1 is 5.5.)
2. To determine the distance of each score from the average, subtract the average from each score as illustrated for Set A in Table 7.2.
3. Remove all negative signs. Mathematicians are not allowed to simply remove negative signs, so they do a few mathematical steps to properly make all the numbers positive, but the effect is the same. So now you have Table 7.3.

Notice that I changed the title of the third column from Difference to Distance. Each of these differences—with the negative signs removed—represents the distance of each score from the average. For example, you see that the score 1 is 4.5 points away from the average of 5.5. You also see that the score 5 is 0.5 points away from the average of 5.5. You now know the distance of every score from the average.

Standard deviation is the average of all these numbers (i.e., the average distance of scores from the average). To calculate the

TABLE 7.2
Subtracting the Average From Each Score

Score	Average	Difference
1	5.5	−4.5
2	5.5	−3.5
3	5.5	−2.5
4	5.5	−1.5
5	5.5	−0.5
6	5.5	0.5
7	5.5	1.5
8	5.5	2.5
9	5.5	3.5
10	5.5	4.5

TABLE 7.3
Distance of Each Score From the Average

Score	Average	Distance
1	5.5	4.5
2	5.5	3.5
3	5.5	2.5
4	5.5	1.5
5	5.5	0.5
6	5.5	0.5
7	5.5	1.5
8	5.5	2.5
9	5.5	3.5
10	5.5	4.5

standard deviation, you calculate the average of the distances (the scores in the third column of Table 7.3). If you add all the distances (= 25) and then divide by the number of scores (10), you get the standard deviation, which is 2.5 (see Table 7.4).

For Set A, the average distance of scores from the average is 2.5, so the standard deviation is 2.5. If you do the same quick calculations for Set B in Table 7.4, you will get a standard deviation (average distance of scores from the average) of 0.5.

The average of Set A and Set B are the same. But the standard deviations of both sets are very different. Standard deviation can tell you how well the average represents the group of scores. The smaller the standard deviation, the better the average represents the whole set of scores. Intuitively (thinking fast), you can tell that 5.5 is more representative of Set B than it is for Set A. Calculating the standard deviation (thinking slow) allows you to measure how well the average represents the scores. In other words, standard deviation measures how much the scores vary. In Microsoft Excel, you can calculate the standard deviation by using the formula =STDEV.P(FirstCell:LastCell).

TABLE 7.4
Standard Deviation of Scores

	A	B
	1	5
	2	6
	3	5
	4	6
	5	5
	6	6
	7	5
	8	6
	9	5
	10	6
Average	**5.5**	**5.5**
Standard Deviation	2.5	0.5

Standard deviation is wonderful for many reasons. First, it is easy to understand after you have used it a few times. Second, it tells you when to trust the average score or when to know that the average is not to be trusted. Third, standard deviation is important for calculating inferential statistics (statistics that make inferences from a sample to a broader population). Again, if there was one thing I would want you to know about statistics beyond averages, it is standard deviation.

Relative Position (z-score)

The third type of descriptive statistic is relative position. Relative position communicates the location of a particular score in relation to the rest of the scores. A common calculation for relative position is the z-score, which indicates the distance of a particular score from the average *in standard deviation units.* So if someone has a z-score of 1.0, that means that the score is exactly 1.0 standard deviation above the average. Put differently, a z-score of 1.0 is 1 (the average distance of scores from the average) above the average. A z-score of −0.5 means that the score is 0.5 standard deviations below the average.

TABLE 7.5
Determining Relative Position by Calculating z-Scores

Score	Average	Difference	z-Score (Difference divided by *SD* of 2.5)
1	5.5	– 4.5	– 1.8
2	5.5	– 3.5	– 1.4
3	5.5	– 2.5	– 1.0
4	5.5	– 1.5	– 0.6
5	5.5	– 0.5	– 0.5
6	5.5	0.5	0.2
7	5.5	1.5	0.6
8	5.5	2.5	1.0
9	5.5	3.5	1.4
10	5.5	4.5	1.8

Once you know the average of a set of scores and the standard deviation of a set of scores, you can calculate the z-score by subtracting the average from each score and dividing the result by the standard deviation. Or you can use Microsoft Excel, as I do. When I do this for Set A, I get the results shown in Table 7.5.

The results in the far right column (the z-scores) tell me how far each score is from the average using standard deviation as the unit of measurement. Why is this useful? Positive scores are above the average, negative scores are below the average, and scores equal to 0 are equal to the average. So z-scores are useful and helpful because standardizing how you measure something allows easy comparisons with what is typical (or average).

This becomes especially useful when you are comparing two things measured in two ways. I experienced this when I became a parent. Every so often, we would take our baby to the doctor and have him weighed and measured. The doctor would tell us the baby's weight in pounds and height in inches. These numbers did not mean anything to us. We really did not care about our baby's weight and height; we wanted to know if our baby was healthy or not. To determine health, the doctor compared the relative position of our baby's weight and height to all other babies in the United States who were the same age in weeks. Now we could understand that our baby was a little taller than average and weighed a little less than average. But there was nothing to worry about. How did the doctor know that there was nothing to worry about? He thought in terms of standard deviations. If our baby was within one standard deviation (z-score of 1 or less), there was nothing to be concerned about. After all, every baby is going to differ in height and weight to some extent. But if our baby was closer to two standard deviations away from the average, then our baby might be far enough from typical to cause concern. Sure enough, this is what happened. Our baby fell two standard deviations below the national average weight and our doctor recommended supplementing calories to make sure he remained healthy. If we knew about z-scores at the time, we could have thought in terms of standard deviations for height and weight using the same numbers for both (because the numbers were in standard deviation units). In other words, we could make comparisons between height and weight even though one is measured in inches and the other in pounds, simply because we were now comparing both scores to their respective averages.

What about in your work in higher education? Any time you need to compare two measurements that use two different scales, you can use z-scores. For example, you might measure sense of belonging on a six-point Likert-type scale. But you also have data that someone else collected on a similar variable, but those data used a five-point Likert scale. If you convert the results of both scales to z-scores, you can make fair comparisons.

In Microsoft Excel, you can calculate z-scores by using the formula =STANDARDIZE(Cell, Input the Average, Input the Standard Deviation). Note that you must precalculate the average and standard deviation so that you can input them into this formula in Excel.

I told you that I would only give you one calculation for each type of descriptive statistic. I need to break that promise here. In addition to z-scores, another excellent way to communicate relative position is percentile. You might be familiar with percentiles if you ever took standardized tests such as the ACT, SAT, or GRE. All three of these tests give you a score on a different scale. For example, you might make a 28 on the ACT, a 1210 on the SAT, and a 300 on the GRE. Those numbers are pretty meaningless unless you can determine how your score relates to others. Therefore, these tests provide you with percentile scores to show you where you stand in relative position to others. If you scored in the 55th percentile, that means you scored better than 55% of test takers. In Microsoft Excel, you can calculate percentiles by using the formula =PERCENTRANK. INC(FirstCell:LastCell, Input Score). By *Input Score*, I mean that you have to write in the particular score that you want the percentile for.

Relationship (Correlation Coefficient)
The fourth type of descriptive statistic is relationship. Please note that although technically a descriptive statistic, the relationship among variables is also the foundation of inferential statistics. Therefore, you may notice that relationship is a type of descriptive statistic, and relationship among variables is one of our four research question categories. The reason for the overlap is that everything we do with statistics involves the relationship among variables. By relationship, I mean the extent to which two variables interact. As one variable goes up, does the other go down? Or perhaps as one goes up, the other goes up also. Or perhaps there is no discernible relationship. Height and weight have a discernible, positive relationship, because as height goes up, weight also tends to go up. Please note that these observations refer to the overall pattern when looking at a large sample, not individual cases. As a whole, height and weight go up together, even though in individual cases you will find exceptions to this pattern.

In student affairs work, you will notice that everyone has a theory about all sorts of relationships among variables. Faculty may believe that as involvement in Greek organizations goes up, GPA goes down. Student affairs professionals who work with Greek organizations may believe that as involvement in Greek life goes up, other variables such as sense of belonging, satisfaction, leadership skills, and retention also go up. There is a big difference between having a theory about a relationship among variables (student affairs fast) and testing a theory using quantitative research and statistics (student affairs slow).

The calculation most commonly used to determine the relationship among variables is the Pearson product-moment correlation coefficient. As you might have guessed, nobody calls it that. Instead, the following are used interchangeably, even if the different terms might have some technical differences: *correlation, correlation coefficient, Pearson correlation, Pearson r, r,* and *regression.* A lowercase *r* is the symbol used to indicate the correlation coefficient. For the rest of this book, I refer to this calculation as simply the *correlation* unless I need to distinguish it further.

A correlation is a number on a scale from -1.0 to $+1.0$ showing the degree to which two variables are related (Vogt & Johnson, 2011). A negative number indicates a negative relationship (as one goes up, the other goes down), and a positive number indicates a positive relationship (as one goes up, the other goes up as well). A number close to zero, whether a positive number or a negative number close to zero, indicates a lack of relationship between the two variables.

When all is said and done, what we want to know in quantitative research and statistics revolves around relationships. Such romantics! As statistics gets more sophisticated and complicated, it is only because more relationships are analyzed. Instead of wondering whether height and weight have a relationship, one might wonder whether height, exercise, socioeconomic status, and distance from the nearest fitness center all have a relationship with weight. Same idea, but more sophisticated. Let's come back to Set A and Set B in Table 7.6.

Although there is no reason to believe that Set A and Set B have a relationship, you can calculate the correlation. In Microsoft Excel, you can calculate correlation by using the function =Pearson(Set 1, Set 2). In doing so, you will find the correlation to be 0.17. This is a positive number close to zero, indicating almost no relationship whatsoever.

You are now wondering what number is big enough to warrant a meaningful relationship. I have two answers to that question. The first is, it depends. I am not trying to be obnoxious here. It really does depend on what the two variables are and what you would expect to see in terms of relationship. If I expected no relationship between Set A and Set B, but the correlation was 0.3, that might seem large

TABLE 7.6
Set A and Set B

A	B
1	5
2	6
3	5
4	6
5	5
6	6
7	5
8	6
9	5
10	6

to me. But if I expected a near-perfect relationship between Set A and Set B, and the correlation was 0.8, then this result might seem small to me. The second answer to the question of what number is big enough to warrant a meaningful relationship is the idea of statistical significance and effect size. I discuss these concepts in the next section on inferential statistics.

There is one last thing to note before moving on: Correlation does not prove causation! Please memorize that phrase. It is vital to your statistical knowledge. Just because two variables are related, even highly related, it does not mean that one variable caused the other variable to occur. This is an important concept to understand. Height and weight are highly correlated, but height does not cause weight. Weight also does not cause height. For example, if you find that student participation in Greek organizations relates to satisfaction, it does not automatically mean that participation in Greek life causes students to be more highly satisfied. What if more highly satisfied students are the ones who choose to participate in Greek life? You do not know which direction the relationship flows. You only know that there is a relationship.

Correlation does not prove causation, but sometimes you can conclude cause and effect because of common sense. Smoking is *other variables*

a good example. There is a high correlation between smoking and lung cancer. Normally I would say that you cannot conclude that smoking causes lung cancer. But lung cancer cannot cause smoking. That does not make sense. So the relationship must flow from smoking to lung cancer in this case. If you cannot discover any hidden variables that could explain this relationship (e.g., smokers happen to also live in places with lots of air pollution), then you can safely conclude that smoking causes lung cancer. This relates to our previous discussion about conclusion validity, the concept that the conclusions you make from your data are logical and valid. Be careful not to ignore conclusion validity simply because you found a relationship between two variables.

How do you use descriptive statistics in your work in student affairs? You must measure something. The most common way I see you measuring something in your work is through the use of scales, as discussed in Chapters 5 and 6. Once you have responses to your survey, it is time to put descriptive statistics to work for you. By adding the responses of a particular scale, you calculate a measurement score for your latent variable. If you remember, my latent variable was faculty support. My instrument was five items, yielding total response scores from 5 to 30. I can use central tendency by calculating the average of these scores. This gives me an estimate of the typical score. Let's say my average faculty support score is 17.5. How accurate or representative is that average? To find out, I need to measure variability by calculating standard deviation. Let's say my standard deviation is 6.1. That means that the average distance of my faculty support scores is 6.1 from the average. Remember that the closer to zero for standard deviation, the less the scores vary. Therefore, I am going to conclude that 6.1 means my scores vary a considerable amount.

I now know central tendency and variability for my faculty support scores. What if I wanted to compare my respondents to each other? This would bring me to relative position and z-scores. By calculating the z-score of each response, I get a new number that tells me how each score relates to the average in terms of standard deviation. If I were to present my research to campus leaders who were interested in faculty support, I might put my respondents into three categories to more clearly convey what is happening with students. The three categories could be low faculty support, some faculty support, and high faculty support. I would then use z-scores to determine which category each student falls into. For example, I could decide that those with a z-score of −1.0 or below (one standard deviation or more below the average) should be classified as low faculty support. I could then have those with a z-score of +1.0 or higher (one standard deviation or more above the average) classified as high faculty support. Those with z-scores greater than −1.0 but lower than +1.0 would be classified as having some faculty support. On my own, determining low, middle, or high is arbitrary—I have no idea what numbers to choose as cutoff scores from one category to the next. But when I use standard deviation and z-scores, I am using how the scores relate to each other as a way to objectively create categories.

I am now ready to determine how variables relate to each other. By determining relationship using correlation, I can think slow about what might be influencing my latent variable. For example, if I had access to the GPA scores or college entrance exam scores of my respondents, I could determine if there was a relationship between college grades and faculty support. Let's say I find a positive correlation of 0.7. Positive correlation means that when college grades go up, faculty support also goes up. This result tells me that there is a relationship between college grades and faculty support, but I now need to be careful not to violate conclusion validity. On the one hand, faculty support helps to improve college grades. On the other hand, perhaps college grades improve faculty support because those who make good grades may know the importance of interacting with faculty, and therefore such students proactively seek relationships with faculty. So even though I know there is a relationship (which is wonderful new information), there are several theories that could explain that relationship. I am welcome to speculate as long as I make it clear that it is nothing more than speculation. I also now have an idea of what to explore with my future research endeavors.

Thus far, you have learned there are two types of statistics: descriptive and inferential. You have also learned there are four types of descriptive statistics, shown in Figure 7.2: central tendency (average), variability (standard deviation), relative position (z-score and percentile), and relationship (correlation). With this foundation of

Figure 7.2. Four types of descriptive statistics.

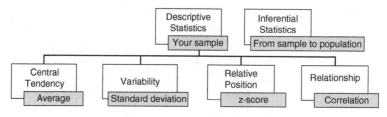

descriptive statistics laid, you are ready to tackle the magic of inferential statistics.

Inferential Statistics

Inferential statistics apply the concepts of descriptive statistics to draw conclusions about a larger population from a smaller sample. It's pretty magical. To understand that magic, you must go one layer deeper in your statistical knowledge. The reason you can accurately make conclusions about people you never collect data from (your population) based on your data (your sample) is that data tend to have certain patterns or shapes on a graph. If you know the shape of your data, then you can do all sorts of amazing tricks that allow you to know about a large group using data from a small group. The shape of your data can be sorted into two main categories, which form the two types of inferential statistics: parametric and nonparametric. Parametric statistics are based on the shape referred to as the *normal distribution.* Nonparametric statistics use data that do not have the normal distribution shape. So when I think of parametric versus nonparametric statistics, I think of normal versus nonnormal data patterns.

Normal Distribution

The normal distribution allows for more powerful statistics. Parametric statistics are more powerful than nonparametric statistics. By powerful, I mean that parametric statistics can detect more sophisticated relationships among variables. A simple way of knowing the distribution of your data is to graph them so that the horizontal axis (x-axis) has the values, and the vertical axis (y-axis) has the frequencies of each value. Because my latent variable of

Figure 7.3. Frequency distribution of faculty support scores.

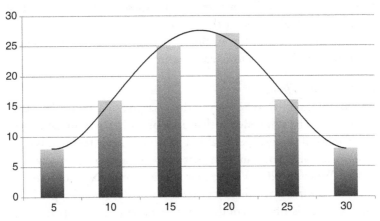

faculty support has a score range from 5 to 30, these are the values on my horizontal axis. The vertical axis represents the number of times respondents have a total faculty support score for each of those values on my horizontal axis. The resulting chart shown in Figure 7.3 is called a *frequency distribution.*

This chart illustrates that of the 100 people who hypothetically responded to my survey, eight people had a faculty support score of five. Moving from left to right, 16 students had a score of 10, 25 students had a score of 15, 27 students had a score of 20, 16 students had a score of 25, and 8 students had the maximum score of 30. The shape of this data looks somewhat like a bell. The *bell curve* is another term for the normal distribution. You may be familiar with the bell curve if you happened to have a teacher who used this to grade a class. Grading on a bell curve means that the teacher will make sure that most of the students get a middle grade, whereas relatively fewer students get low grades or high grades. When your data have a shape similar to this distribution, you can conduct parametric statistics.

Charting your data like this can get very tedious, however, especially when you have large sample sizes. So statisticians use statistical software to judge whether their data have a normal distribution. They also use sophisticated mathematical techniques to make adjustments when their data do not have a normal distribution. This is all right and proper, but I am going to allow you to cheat and skip these techniques for now. Someday, you will get so advanced and sophisticated you will want to conduct these calculations. At that point, you will also scoff at the elementary nature of this book and how it is now so beneath you. But until then, let's cheat! The central limit theorem is what allows you to cheat.

Central Limit Theorem

A theorem is similar to a theory in the sense that it is a way of explaining things. The difference is that a theorem is a way of explaining mathematical things, specifically. The central limit theorem is a big deal. Otherwise, you can trust that I would not bother you with it. In fact, Wheelan (2013) refers to it as the LeBron James of statistics.

The central limit theorem states that when samples get larger than 30, the distribution of the sample will be a normal distribution. Allow me to break that down and explain why this is so amazing. Normal distributions allow you to conduct parametric statistics, which are more powerful (sensitive) than nonparametric statistics. According to the central limit theorem, when your sample becomes larger than 30, it will take on a normal distribution and allow you to use these more powerful statistical methods. Thirty is not a large number, and it is not difficult to get a sample size of 30 people. The larger the sample, the more likely it is to take on the shape of a normal distribution. So even though you should conduct statistical tests to test whether your distribution is normal, you could also rely on the central limit theorem and assume normality if your sample is larger than 30. There are benefits and drawbacks to this approach. The drawback is that you could be wrong, and it is better to be safe than sorry. The advantage is that you do not need to be bogged down by things such as testing normality when you are just learning statistics. You can safely cheat and skip this step (based on this theorem) and learn how to check for it when you are farther along on your statistical journey. I give you permission to do so.

The 68-95-99 Rule for Normal Distributions

When you know the shape of your data, and when your data follow a normal distribution, you can also apply what is commonly referred to as the 68-95-99 rule. Standard deviation, if you recall, is the average distance of scores from the average. The 68-95-99 rule states that 68% of your data will be within one standard deviation of the average in a normal distribution (34% of the data is one standard deviation below the average, and 34% of the data is one standard deviation above the average). As follows, 95% of your data is within two standard deviations, and 99% of your data is within three standard deviations. So practically all the data fall within three standard deviations of the average. Earlier, I decided to use z-scores to determine those students with low, middle, and high faculty support. I decided a z-score of −1.0 or below would be low faculty support and a z-score of +1.0 would be high faculty support. Using the 68-95-99 rule, I now know that 68% of my respondents would be categorized as the middle group (because this is the percentage within one standard deviation of my average). This leaves 16% in the low faculty support group and 16% in the high faculty support group (because 32% is left and 32% divided by two is 16%). This rule helps you connect standard deviations to percentages of your sample. Thinking in these terms is also a gateway to understanding statistical significance.

Statistical Significance
The purpose of inferential statistics is to draw conclusions (inferences) about a population from a relatively small sample. Step 1 of this process is to determine relationships among variables in your sample. If relationships are found, Step 2 of this process is to determine if that relationship found in your sample also exists in your population. You cannot know with absolute certainty anything about people you do not collect data from (your population). But with inferential statistics, you can know something about people you do not study (your population) with a surprising amount of certainty because of what you know about people you did study (your sample). This brings up the following question: How certain do we need to be before we can make appropriate claims about a population from a sample? The answer: 95% certain.

When you can say that you are 95% certain that relationships found in your sample would also be found in your population, you have statistical significance. Statistical significance tends to be the first concern when it comes to the results of a statistical analysis. In other words, it is the first thing you look for in your statistical output. In statistics you never prove anything. Instead, you think in terms of probabilities. If there is a 5% chance (or less) that your claim that relationships in your sample also exist in the population is wrong, the scholarly world can live with that. This probability of your being wrong about a claimed relationship among variables is known as the *probability level* or p-*value.* If the p-value is above .05 (in decimal format), you do not have statistical significance because there is less than a 95% probability of your claim being correct. If the p-value is less than or equal to .05, your findings are statistically significant.

Why is 95% confidence the standard? Why not 90% or 99%? It is completely based on tradition. Over time, researchers felt that a 10% chance of being wrong was too risky. By contrast, demanding only a 1% chance of being wrong felt too stringent. So eventually a 5% chance of being wrong became the standard. This is an important point. In practical, common sense terms, the difference between being 94% confident and 95% confident is meaningless. Yet, by academic standards, one would mean you do not have statistical significance, and the other would mean that you do have statistical significance. That is a little silly, but I guess people had to draw the line somewhere. If you desire to publish your findings, this is basically an unbreakable standard that you must follow. But if you are conducting research for the good of your campus without seeking to publish, you can use common sense. You could simply state that you are 94% confident that what you found in your sample also exists in your population. If my results showed me that I could be 90% confident of the relationships found, I would think to myself that it's not as confident as I would like to be, but it seems there could really be something going on here. I wonder if having a larger sample in my next round of research would allow me to be even more confident next time? I can think in these terms because I understand statistical significance. You can think in these terms because you now understand it as well.

Effect Size

Statistical significance is overrated; effect size is underrated. Conceptually, people often mistakenly combine the two. If statistical significance is the first thing you want to know after your analysis of inferential statistics, effect size is the second. I could make a case that effect size is even more important than statistical significance. Statistical significance is whether you can be 95% confident that a relationship or difference among variables found in a sample will

also be found in the population. Effect size is how much of a relationship or difference is found. Statistical significance answers the
question of if. Effect size answers the question of how much.

Effect size is a big deal. Who really cares whether there is a significant relationship if the degree of the relationship is so small that
it has no practical value? But if there is a decent effect size, then you
know that your finding has meaningful significance in addition to
statistical significance. If you have a moderate effect size, but you do
not have statistical significance, it means there is a real difference in
your sample, but you cannot (with adequate confidence) infer that
finding in your population. I must admit that interpreting effect size
is not as clear cut as statistical significance. This is for two reasons:
There are multiple methods of calculating effect size, and there is a
lack of a clear standard for what is a good effect size.

There are multiple methods for calculating and reporting effect
size, depending on the specific statistical analysis you conduct.
Because correlations are so prominent in statistics, I will first teach
you the effect size commonly used with correlations. The proper
name for a correlation, if you remember, is *Pearson product-moment
correlation coefficient.* The proper name for its corresponding effect
size is *Pearson correlation coefficient squared* (or coefficient of determination). This is not a trick name. The effect size for a correlation
is calculated by squaring the correlation. As a quick reminder, a correlation is a number showing the degree to which two variables are
related on a scale from -1.0 to $+1.0$. The letter r is used to designate
a correlation. Once you have that correlation, you square it (multiply
the number by itself) to get the effect size. So if my correlation (r) is
0.39, my effect size (r^2) is 0.15 (because $0.39 * 0.39 = 0.15$). Here is
the real practical use of effect size: your r^2 represents the proportion
of variance that one variable explains for another variable. (I use
an asterisk in the formulas in this book to indicate multiplication.)
Effect size, calculated as r^2, allows you to think in terms of percentages. In other words, an effect size of 0.15 means that one variable is
predicting, explaining, or influencing 15% of another variable. An
example will help to clarify this idea further.

There is no clear standard for a good or bad effect size. There is
no arbitrary cutoff as there is for statistical significance. Therefore,
context really matters. For example, the SAT is a controversial college entrance exam. Some colleges require it, whereas others choose

not to use it in admissions decisions. Those who support the use of the SAT and those who argue against it use effect size to defend their arguments. You will find different effect sizes for the SAT from different sources, but let's say the effect size is 15%. That would mean that SAT scores account for 15% of the variability in first-year GPA (first-year college GPA is the variable the SAT predicts). On the one hand, 15% is small, leaving 85% of what influences first-year GPA unaccounted for. On the other hand, trying to make predictions regarding the academic success of young adults is extremely difficult, and having knowledge about 15% of that puzzle could be extremely helpful. Therefore, in some sense, effect size is in the eye of the beholder.

Another method to calculate effect size is to put it in terms of standard deviation (the average distance of scores from the average). This standardized effect size is known as Cohen's *d*, often used in experiments and quasi-experiments in which you are comparing a group receiving a treatment to a control group that does not receive the treatment. To calculate effect size in this manner, take the average score of the treatment group, subtract the average score of the control group, and divide by the standard deviation of the control group. Or you could do what I do and search the Internet for an effect size calculator. The result you get represents the difference between the two groups as expressed in standard deviation units.

Again, you must remember that context matters when it comes to effect size. For example, sometimes researchers substitute students' GPAs with their self-reported GPAs. Because researchers do not always have access to students' GPAs, they instead ask the students to tell the researchers their GPAs. Some scholars have studied how well self-reported GPAs correlate with actual GPAs (Caskie, Sutton, & Eckhardt, 2014). Let's say the effect size between self-reported GPA and actual GPA is 0.8, meaning that a self-reported GPA accounts for 80% of the variance in the actual GPA. Usually, an effect size of 0.8 would be extremely high, but in this case I would argue it is low. Although students are doing an okay job telling the truth about their GPAs, the two variables are not close enough to completely substitute self-reported GPA for actual GPA.

Once you understand effect size, I think it is important for you to think of statistical significance and effect size independently from one another. This is not something people regularly do. From my observations, people first determine if there is statistical significance. If there is statistical significance, then they might look at effect size as a second step. Instead of taking this Step 1, Step 2 approach, I suggest you examine statistical significance and effect size together. Doing so will make you a more sophisticated thinker. It may be the case that your results are not statistically significant, but you have a medium or large effect size. That still means something. As mentioned earlier, it means that a medium or large effect was found in your sample, but you cannot say with 95% confidence that this effect would also be found in your population. Perhaps a larger sample (in your next round of research) would result in finding statistical significance. On the flip side, if you have statistical significance, but you do not have a meaningful effect size, you can translate your findings as having no practical significance.

Even though there is no clear standard for a good effect size, Cohen (1988, 1992) helpfully offers suggestions. I provide guidelines for effect size in Tables 7.7 and 7.8.

The first column in Table 7.7 displays the correlation between two variables. The second column displays the effect size,

TABLE 7.7
Effect Size Guideline

Correlation (r)	Effect Size (r^2)	% That One Variable Explains of Another	General Effect Size Category	Minimum Sample Size to Detect Effect
0.1	0.01	1%	Small	783
0.2	0.04	4%	Small	
0.3	0.09	9%	Medium	85
0.4	0.16	16%	Medium	
0.5	0.25	25%	Large	28
0.6	0.36	36%	Large	
0.7	0.49	49%	Large	
0.8	0.64	64%	Large	
0.9	0.81	81%	Large	

Note. Based on Cohen (1988).

TABLE 7.8
Effect Size Guidelines When Comparing Groups

Cohen's value of d (in standard deviation units)	General effect size category	Mayhew and colleagues (2016)
.20	Small	.15
.50	Medium	.30
.80	Large	.50

Note. Based on Cohen (1992) and Mayhew, Rokenbach, Bowman, Seifert, Wolniak, Pascarella, and Terenzini (2016).

calculated by squaring the correlation. The third column shows the effect size as a percentage rather than a decimal. The fourth column shows Cohen's (1988) general categorization of small, medium, and large effect sizes. The fifth column represents the minimum sample size needed to detect an effect of that size (more on that column later). In *How College Affects Students*, Mayhew, Rokenbach, Bowman, Seifert, Wolniak, Pascarella, and Terenzini (2016, pp. 16–20) provide effect size suggestions, particularly focusing on research with college students. I highly recommend you read those pages. As a comparison to Table 7.7, here are their category suggestions for effect size: small = .06, medium = .12, large = .20).

For Cohen's d (effect size in standard deviation units), Cohen (1992) makes the suggestions shown in Table 7.8. This type of effect size is used when comparing groups. Mayhew and colleagues (2016) suggest the following categories for effect size when comparing groups: small = .15, medium = .30, large = .50). These suggestions convey that when groups differ from one another by just one-third to one-half of a standard deviation, it is a noticeable difference.

So far, we have covered four types of descriptive statistics and four important aspects of inferential statistics. Figure 7.4 displays our knowledge thus far. There are a couple of concepts we need to cover before moving forward.

Sample Size
Sample size is extremely important in inferential statistics. According to the column on the far right of Table 7.7, if there is a large effect, impact, or influence between two variables (e.g., one variable

Figure 7.4. Four types of descriptive statistics and four aspects of inferential statistics.

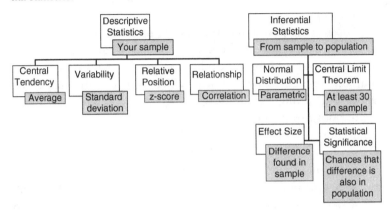

accounts for 25% of the variance in another variable), you would need only 28 respondents for your statistical analyses to detect that effect. But if there is only a medium effect (e.g., one variable accounts for just 9% of another variable), you need a larger sample to detect that effect (a sample of 85 instead of just 28). If there is only a small impact between two variables (e.g., 1%), your sample must be at least 783 to detect that effect (Cohen, 1988). The moral of this story is that as your sample gets larger, the chances of detecting statistical significance increases, but the needed size of effect decreases. Therefore, larger sample sizes tend to increase power. The central limit theorem states that randomly selected samples of at least 30 will have a normal distribution. But sample sizes larger than 30 are very helpful for reaching statistical significance and for detecting smaller relationships among variables. Thus, it is worth the effort to get as large a sample as practically possible.

Variables

Up to this point, I have not spent much time explaining variables. I have mentioned that a variable is something that varies in quantity or quality. It is important to understand there are different types of variables. These different types are used in specific statistical methods. In other words, some statistical methods were created just for a specific type of variable. The three categories for variables I give you are used in IBM SPSS. I am also using the names for the categories that IBM SPSS uses (although there are many other names for each of these categories, which makes statistics as hard to learn as possible).

The three types of variables are nominal, ordinal, and scale. When you hear nominal, think *name*. Nominal variables represent categories, and examples include race, gender, student organization, and residential community. When you hear ordinal, think *order*. With ordinal variables, you use numbers, but these numbers are not measuring something; rather, they represent an order or ranking. For example, student classification of year is ordinal. *First-year, sophomore, junior, senior*, and *graduate student* represent categories, and these categories have an order to them. Sophomore comes before junior, for example. When you hear scale, think *measurement scale*. These variables use numbers on a continuum to measure the quantity or quality of something. Examples include GPA, the number of organizations a student belongs to, and the summed responses to items in your latent variable scale.

As we move into the next chapter on statistical approaches, I want to make sure you understand these three categories of variables. Nominal is categorical, ordinal is order, and scale is a measurement scale. This knowledge will be essential in moving forward with choosing a statistical approach.

Moving Forward

In the next chapter, I take each of our four categories of quantitative research questions and connect it to at least one statistical method. When you combine knowledge of the four types of descriptive statistics with knowledge of the four types of questions you can answer with inferential statistics, you have a solid foundation of statistical knowledge (see Figure 7.5). I highly recommend you use the following review questions to identify the parts of this chapter that have not yet stuck in your mind. Please review those parts before moving on to the next chapter. In the subsequent chapters, I discuss a popular statistical analysis for each of the four types of quantitative research questions.

Figure 7.5. Categories and methods for descriptive and inferential statistics.

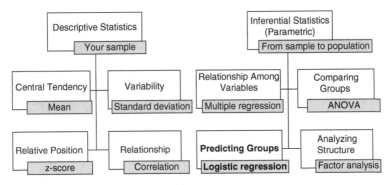

Review Questions From This Chapter

The following are review questions you can use to test yourself. When you test yourself, you force yourself to recall information, and the act of recalling leads to better and deeper learning.

- What is the difference between the two types of statistics: descriptive and inferential?
- What are the four types of descriptive statistics?
- What is one primary way of calculating each of the four types of descriptive statistics?
- What is the normal distribution?
- What is the difference between parametric and nonparametric statistics?
- What does the central limit theorem state, and how is it helpful?
- What does the 68-95-99 rule state, and how is it helpful?
- What is statistical significance?
- What is effect size, and how does it differ from statistical significance?
- What are the two primary ways of calculating effect size?
- How does the size of your sample affect your results?
- What are the three categories of variables, and how do they differ?

8

STATISTICAL APPROACH FOR THE QUESTION OF RELATIONSHIP

Dana Lee is interested in the leadership development of college students. In her job, she spends time developing students' leadership skills through programs she creates. However, she does not have any real sense about whether her programs make a difference in the leadership of students. Dana Lee has spent time with the literature, reading some journal articles on the leadership development of college students. She begins by reading the introduction to each article. When she gets to the methods, she tries to understand, gets bored pretty quickly, and skips to the conclusions. The conclusions are helpful, but she is not able to make connections among what was done, what was found, and the resulting conclusions. And she certainly does not feel any closer to knowing how to conduct research on leadership development herself. Dana Lee knows that she can create her own scale to measure leadership or use a scale already developed by others. But when she administers such a scale, what does she do with the results? What question is she answering? How can she use research and statistics to give her useful information that can improve the experiences of her students? Dana Lee is ready to take this step.

Overview

This book offers four categories of research questions (see Chapter 4) you can ask involving quantitative research and statistics. This chapter provides a more in-depth explanation of the first of those four categories (relationship among variables). Specifically, I discuss statistical approaches for measuring the degree of relationship among two or more variables. (The other categories, comparing groups, predicting groups, and analyzing structure, are each discussed in subsequent chapters.) I only discuss parametric approaches (using a sample with a normal distribution) for each of the four categories of questions. I stick with parametric approaches because they are more powerful, more commonly seen in the research literature, and should be appropriate for your use as long as you have a decent sample size (minimum of 30 but the more, the better).

My purpose is to help you understand these approaches conceptually. Yes, I want you to know how to do them yourself, but I will not take you step-by-step through those processes. There are already lots of books that can do that. The authors of those books try to explain the approaches and then try to tell you how to conduct the analyses. I think that is too much at one time. This chapter will help you understand what these approaches do, when to use them, and how to interpret the results. If I can lay a solid foundation of conceptual understanding, then learning the steps later for any particular statistical software will be relatively quick and easy. It is my job to get you to take that initial step.

Figure 8.1. Overview of descriptive and inferential statistics.

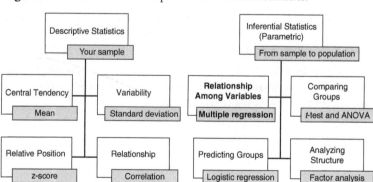

I start each section with a description of the parametric (normal distribution) approach. I then select a research article from a higher education or student affairs journal and use that article to walk you through the approach. Whenever possible, I will use a research article from my own scholarship enabling me to speak about what was done and why it was done. The chart in Figure 8.1 displays an overview of descriptive and inferential statistics. You should know the left side of the chart. I discuss the right side of the chart in this chapter and in chapters 9 through 11.

Relationship Among Variables

When we learned about the four types of descriptive statistics in Chapter 7 (central tendency, variability, relative position, and relationship), we learned that variability is how much scores vary. When you think about two variables, instead of only thinking about variance (standard deviation), you can also think about covariance. With covariance, when one variable changes, the other variable changes as well (either in the same direction or in the opposite direction). The concept of covariance leads to another type of descriptive statistic we covered—relationship.

The problem with covariance is that it is not standardized (converted to a standard scale). Correlation (corelationship) measures covariance but in a standardized way that communicates relationship on a scale from −1.0 (perfectly negative relationship) to +1.0 (perfectly positive relationship). You may remember from the previous chapter that the symbol for correlation is r, which stands for *regression*, another term for correlation.

When you hear regression, think correlation (corelationship). Regression is a type of correlation in which you try to predict the outcome of one variable from another (Vogt & Johnson, 2011). Almost everything we do in statistics is based on the relationships among variables. In fact, the other three categories of research questions (comparing groups, predicting groups, and analyzing structure) are really just variations of using regression analysis. So if you understand regression, you grasp the foundation of inferential statistics.

The good news is that correlations and regressions are really easy to do and easy to interpret. You should do them all the time just for fun. In fact, I just did one. While thinking of an example of how to use a correlation in your work, I thought about a question I might be interested in for my work. I oversee admissions for my graduate program in higher education and student affairs and my doctoral program in higher education studies and leadership. The GRE, which is required for admission into these programs, has three sections: verbal, quantitative, and analytical. I noticed that the analytical section of the GRE gets discussed relatively little in comparison to the verbal and quantitative sections. The verbal and quantitative sections both have standardized scores ranging from 130 to 170. The analytical section, however, is different. It is not multiple choice but is a response in the form of an essay that is graded by a trained reader. The scale for this section is 0 to 6 in increments of 0.5.

One question that has lingered in the back of my mind is how much the verbal and analytical sections of the GRE overlap. Are these sections evaluating the same skills? Is the analytical section necessary? Does it add any value that is not accounted for by the verbal section? One faculty member on my admissions committee cares deeply about the analytical section scores of applicants, but others hardly pay attention. If I want to answer this question by thinking slow, I can use a correlation. The process is relatively simple. I put all GRE verbal scores in one column of an Excel spreadsheet. I then put all corresponding analytical scores in another column. By *corresponding* I mean that I make sure each row represents the same person (e.g., David's verbal score is on the same row as David's analytical score). In a third column, I pick a cell and type in the formula: =PEARSON(scores in column 1, scores in column 2). Excel uses the term *Pearson* because it is technically a Pearson product-moment correlation coefficient. When I conduct this correlation, I get $r = 0.52$.

On a scale of 0 to 1, 0.52 is right in the middle. Is this good or bad? Excel does not provide me with statistical significance. I could determine statistical significance by using statistical software, but I actually do not care about statistical significance because I am not trying to make inferences from this sample to a population. In this case I am only interested in the sample itself. To help me answer the question of whether 0.52 is good or bad, I square 0.52 to get the effect size. When I conduct this calculation, I get $r^2 = 0.27$. I now know that 27% of the variance in analytical scores can be explained by verbal scores. Generally speaking, this is a large effect size. But statistics will not do the thinking for me in relation to what is a good or bad effect size. Instead, statistics will provide me with information to help me to think slow. Although verbal scores account for 27% of the variance in analytical scores, verbal scores likewise do not explain 73% of the variance (100% − 27% = 73%). I interpret this to mean that there is a decent overlap between the two sections but not enough to rule out the usefulness of the analytical section. Therefore, I will continue to look at analytical scores alongside verbal scores. There are three things I hope are apparent to you through this example: You can learn interesting information through correlation or regression, learning it is relatively easy, and you do not necessarily need fancy statistical software to learn it.

Multiple Regression

As you use correlations and become comfortable with them, you will begin to hunger for the next step. A correlation is beautiful because it is simple. With simplicity, however, comes a reduction of information. When you want more information, you must conduct a more sophisticated approach. Multiple regression is the most frequently used statistical procedure because it provides a balance between simplicity and complexity. It gives you more information than a simple regression, but it is not so complex that you feel overwhelmed by statistical jargon.

A multiple regression is similar to a simple regression in the sense that they both have one dependent (outcome) variable. Therefore, the *multiple* part of multiple regression has to do with the number of independent (predictor) variables. Whereas a simple regression has one independent variable, a multiple regression has multiple independent variables. Multiple regression is useful because it develops an equation that takes into account multiple independent variables to predict a dependent variable.

Typically the independent variables and the dependent variable in multiple regression must be scale variables (measured on a continuum). The number of times a student participates in a program is a scale variable. College entrance test scores are scale variables. A college GPA is a scale variable. Also, summed scores on a scale that you create represent a scale variable. Let's use this last case as an example.

When we created a scale together in Chapter 6, I developed an instrument to try to measure the latent variable of faculty support. Assuming that my scale is reliable with all five items, I can add the responses of those items to create a single score that measures faculty support. I now have two choices. I can use this faculty support variable as an independent (predictor) variable or I can use it as a dependent (outcome) variable. If I were to use faculty support as an independent variable in a multiple regression, it would then become one of two or more variables meant to predict another dependent variable. I could use faculty support as an independent variable along with college entrance test scores (e.g., the SAT or ACT) to determine if those variables can combine to predict the dependent variable of GPA. By contrast, I might have other variables I want to use to try to predict faculty support (with faculty support now serving as my dependent variable). A sample research question using multiple regression could be, To what extent do race, gender, living on campus, and college entrance test scores predict perceived faculty support by students? You may have noticed that in this question I use variables (see Chapter 7, p. 127) that are scale (measured on a continuum) and nominal (categorical). You can use categorical variables in a multiple regression, but there is a trick to doing so.

Using Nominal (Categorical) Variables

A limitation of multiple regression is that the independent variables and the dependent variable should be scale variables, which means they are measured on a continuum. This is unfortunate because you may be interested in the influence of nominal (categorical) variables as well. Fortunately, there is a work-around that allows you to use nominal variables as independent variables in a multiple regression. If you can limit a nominal variable to two categories, and if you code those two categories as 0 and 1, you can create a *dummy variable* that can be used as an independent variable in a multiple regression. The reason this works is that assigning categories of 0 and 1 basically creates a variable that calculates how often one of the categories occurs. In my example, I am interested in the influences of race, gender, living on campus, and college entrance test scores as possible predictors (independent variables) of faculty support (dependent variable). I have four independent variables, but only one of them is a scale variable (college entrance test scores). I can use the other three as independent variables in my multiple regression as long as I can code each variable in two categories. For race, this could mean giving a 0 to White students and a 1 to students of color. For gender, I could use 0 for females and 1 for males. For living on campus, I could use 0 for not living on campus and 1 for living on campus. If I had 100 respondents, and if 38 of them were students of color, then 38 would have the code of 1 in my spreadsheet, and 62 would have the code of 0 (the White students). When the software averages all those 0s and 1s, it comes out to .38, indicating that 38% of students are students of color. The multiple regression can then use these 0s and 1s to determine the influence each catagory has on faculty support.

Three Approaches of Multiple Regression

The three primary ways of conducting a multiple regression are standard, hierarchical, and stepwise. These three versions describe different approaches for analyzing your independent variables. With standard multiple regression, you enter all independent variables into the calculations (referred to as the *model*) at the same time, thereby allowing the software to address them all together and produce results. This is a common and safe way to conduct multiple regression. And in some cases, this approach makes the most sense. But in other cases, you may want to specify the order that the independent variables are entered into the calculations. By doing so, you can more easily determine how much certain variables (the variables you put in later) add to your prediction power. When you specify the order, you conduct a hierarchical multiple regression. In this approach, the independent variables believed to be most influential are entered first, and subsequent independent variables are added to determine the specific amount of variance they each may add. Stepwise multiple regression allows the software to determine the order that the independent variables are entered into the calculations.

Sample Size for Multiple Regression

Providing a sample size goal for any statistical approach is a difficult thing to do. There is a reason that when asked about desirable sample sizes, people who know their stuff unhelpfully say, it depends. But I also know that you want guidelines. I know this because I wanted guidelines, and I appreciated those who risked themselves to go beyond the it depends safe answer. Thanks to the central limit theorem, we already know that sample sizes greater than 30 begin to form a normal distribution, which is a must for all the inferential statistics I discuss in this book. I have also established that when it comes to sample size, the more the better.

Personally, I have found that a sample size of 100 seems to reach a threshold of performing well statistically; however, sometimes you can get away with smaller samples. Tabachnick and Fidell (2007) suggest two possible formulas for determining a minimum sample size. The first formula is to take your number of independent variables, multiply by 8, and add 50. So with my four independent variables in my example of faculty support, I would need a sample size of at least 82 (4 x 8 = 32; 32 + 50 = 82). The second formula is to take the number of independent variables and add 104. In this case, the minimum sample size for four independent variables would be 108 (4 + 104 = 108). They suggest doing both calculations and going with the higher of the two numbers for your minimum sample size. You can see how their suggestions align with my suggested threshold of 100. You can also see how an increase in independent variables requires an increase in sample size.

Interpreting Results

Statistical software provides so much information after conducting an analysis that it is overwhelming. The software does nothing to tell you what is extremely important versus what is nice information to know. I do not think I would do you a favor if I told you what everything was and what it meant. Rather, I am going to act as your filter. This book emphasizes what I think is most important to know. When you have this knowledge, you will be ready to learn the rest with another statistics book. When interpreting results, you need to know statistical significance, effect size, and the gift a particular statistical approach gives you.

Statistical Significance

As a reminder, statistical significance has to do with whether results you find in your sample can also be inferred in your population. When there is a 95% chance or higher of making that inference correctly, you have statistical significance (*p*-value is less than or equal to 0.05). Every statistical procedure uses a particular test of significance. In multiple regression, the test of significance is called an *F*-test. You can find the results of this test in the ANOVA (analysis of variance) table of results. This table provides you with the *p*-value. If you are reading a journal article, the authors will most likely tell you the *p*-value for the model. If the number is less than or equal to 0.05, then the results are considered statistically significant.

Effect Size

Statistical significance deals with whether you can make inferences from your sample to your population. Effect size, by contrast, is not about if your variables relate to each other significantly but rather how much your variables relate to each other. In multiple regression, you care about the effect size of your overall model (the whole multiple regression) and individual independent variables. This is an important point. You are asking not only if your combination of independent variables can predict your dependent variable but also about the strength of the predictive power for each independent variable.

R^2. The correlation of a simple regression (one independent variable and one dependent variable) is denoted by *r*. The correlation of a multiple regression (also called a multiple correlation) is denoted by a capital *R*. Likewise, the effect size is labeled as R^2 for a multiple correlation instead of r^2. When examining *R*, you are gauging the relationship between a combination of your independent variables and your dependent variable. Generally speaking, 0.1 is a small relationship, 0.3 is a medium relationship, and 0.5 is a large relationship. Squaring your *R* (to calculate R^2) will give you the effect size or the degree of variance of your dependent variable explained by the independent variables in terms of a percentage. So an R^2 of 0.28 means that the combination of your independent variables explains, accounts for, or predicts 28% of the variance in your dependent variable.

B weights and beta weights. Once you have a sense of what the overall multiple regression model does, it is time to examine the effect of individual independent variables. To find the effect of each independent variable, the statistical software will give you unstandardized regression coefficients and standardized regression coefficients. Unstandardized scores (also called *B* weights) are always interpreted based on the unit you are using to measure. So if you are using weight in pounds as one of your independent variables, the unstandardized regression coefficient will give you an effect size also using pounds. By contrast, the standardized regression coefficient (also called beta weights) gives you the effect size in terms of standard deviation, thereby allowing you to compare effects even when comparing different measurement units.

For example, if one of my independent variables is weight in pounds, and another is height in inches, I cannot compare their effects based on unstandardized regression coefficients (because I cannot really compare the magnitude of pounds versus the magnitude of inches). However, if I look at my beta weights (standardized regression coefficients), I might see that the effect size of weight is 0.3 standard deviation, but the effect size of height is 0.6 standard deviation (revealing that the impact of height on the dependent variable is greater than that of weight).

A helpful feature of multiple regression is that it displays the effect of one variable while also controlling for the effect of all the other variables. Therefore, when you analyze the effect of a single independent variable, you have removed any influence from other independent variables. This makes comparisons between independent variables clean and reliable.

The Gift of Multiple Regression

Every statistical approach provides you with a gift. For multiple regression, that gift is an equation. In essence, a multiple regression charts your data and calculates the best fitting line that can describe your data. This line can be described as an equation, and this equation can be used to make future predictions. The following is the general equation for a multiple regression:

Dependent Variable = B_0 + (B_1 * Independent Variable 1, + B_2 * Independent Variable 2, . . .) + error

I try to avoid formulas in this book, but this one is important and useful. Let's break it down using my faculty support scale. The equation is calculating (predicting) the value of my dependent variable, which in my case is faculty support. Let's pretend I used a multiple regression with the independent variables of race, gender, living on campus, and college entrance test scores to predict my dependent variable of faculty support. In my results, the output gives me a value called the *constant* (represented by B_0 in the preceding formula). The output also gives me B weights (unstandardized regression coefficients) for each of my independent variables (represented by B_1 and B_2 in the preceding formula). All I need to do is plug the constant and the B weights into the equation. Doing so gives me the following:

Faculty Support = *Constant* + (*B weight for race* * Race, + *B weight for gender* * Gender, + *B weight for living on campus* * Living on Campus, + *B weight for college entrance test scores* * College Entrance Test Scores) + error

The term *error* is simply a way to indicate that my equation will not be perfect in its prediction. I can now take students for whom I know their race, gender, whether they live on campus, and their college entrance test scores and calculate a predicted level of faculty support they will experience. Keep in mind that some of these independent variables may not turn out to be significant predictors. In that case, the multiple regression kicks those independent variables out and only shows you those that remain as significant predictors. Therefore, even though I plugged in four independent variables into the multiple regression analysis, my final equation could use all four independent variables or three, two, or just one.

Multiple Regression in Use

For each statistical approach I discuss, I provide an example from research. For multiple regression, I describe a study led by one of my former graduate students, Ah Ra Cho. Ah Ra knew I was interested in the competencies of student affairs professionals and in collaborations between academic affairs and student affairs. She had a similar interest. Ah Ra's assistantship was helping to lead the Global Living-Learning Community, a partnership between the Department of

Modern Languages and Cultures and the residence life department in student affairs. Therefore, she experienced firsthand the challenges of leading and managing such collaborative partnerships.

I was in the midst of creating a scale to measure every competency listed by ACPA and NASPA (2010). I felt that collaboration with academic affairs was a competency missing from the list, and Ah Ra certainly agreed. So we created a couple of scales to add to my survey. One scale measured the collaborative competency level of student affairs professionals, and the other scale measured perceptions of a culture conducive to collaboration. Our goals were to better understand predictors of the measured skills needed to form partnerships with academic affairs and measure perceptions of a collaborative institutional culture and its influence on skills (Cho & Sriram, 2016). We chose multiple regression because we wanted to see if and how a variety of independent variables (perceptions of a collaborative culture and demographic variables) predicted our dependent variable (collaborative competency level). Specifically, our demographic predictor variables consisted of gender, age of professional, years in higher education administration, years at current institution, years in current position, highest degree earned (categorized as no graduate degree, master's degree, or terminal degree), whether professional had a degree in higher education or student affairs, and level of current position (categorized as entry level, midlevel, or senior administrator). Notice that we created two scales for this research. We used one scale as an independent variable (perceptions of a collaborative culture) and another scale as a dependent variable (collaborative competency level).

When analyzing our results, we were interested in evaluating statistical significance and effect size. For our results to be statistically significant, we would need a p-value less than or equal to 0.05; ours was less than 0.001. Of the 10 independent variables we had in our model, only three were significant. This means that the multiple regression kept three of our independent variables and tossed out the other seven. The three significant independent variables were whether the individual had a terminal degree, whether the individual was a senior administrator versus an entry-level administrator, and the perceptions of the institutional collaborative culture. Remember, having such a low p-value for our multiple regression means that the chances of our finding our results randomly is very low. Therefore, what we found in our sample most likely exists in the population as well. A lower p-value does not mean that our results are more meaningful than a higher p-value, however. For level of impact, we must turn to effect size.

In multiple regression, three aspects of effect size are important: overall model effect size (R^2), individual independent variable effect size in an unstandardized format (B weights), and individual independent variable effect size in a standardized format (beta weights). For the overall model, our R^2 was 0.313. This means that our model (the three remaining independent variables) predicted 31.3% of the variance in collaborative competency. That's really cool! On the one hand, that leaves 68.7% unaccounted for. But on the other hand, the ability to predict a third of what contributes to collaborative competency levels is a big deal. Table 8.1 displays the B weights and beta weights for each of the significant independent variables.

Let's go through this step-by-step to understand together what these results mean. Remember that all three of these independent variables are statistically significant predictors of the dependent variable (collaborative competency level). Statistical significance means that the chances of the influences of these independent variables not actually being found in the population are really low. Table 8.1 represents effect size, how much of an influence each of these independent variables has on collaborative competency level.

Remember, B weights are unstandardized. This means they tell you how much your dependent variable goes up (or down if the B weight is negative) when the independent variable increases by one unit. But we must be careful in our interpretation. Two of our

TABLE 8.1

B **Weights and Beta Weights for Predicting Collaboration as a Competency**

Variable	B Weights	Beta Weights
Terminal degree	3.21	0.24
Senior-level position	2.88	0.23
Perceptions of a collaborative institutional culture	0.52	0.33

independent variables are nominal (categorical), and one is scale (measured on a continuum). So for terminal degree, we gave each person with a terminal degree a 1 and each person without a terminal degree a 0 (Cho & Sriram, 2016). Therefore, we interpret the *B* weight to mean that when terminal degree goes up by one (goes from no terminal degree to having a terminal degree), collaborative competency level goes up by 3.21 points on our six-point Likert-type scale. Similarly, when senior-level position goes up by one unit (from not in a senior-level position to holding a senior-level position), collaborative competency goes up by 2.88 points on our scale. So for categorical variables, going up by one unit means switching from one category to the other.

Interpreting the effects of perceptions of a collaborative institutional culture is a bit more intuitive. In this case, we have a scale variable as an independent variable (perceptions of a collaborative institutional culture) and a scale variable as the dependent variable (collaborative competency level). So the *B* weight means that when perceptions of a collaborative institutional culture go up by one point on the six-point Likert-type scale, collaborative competency level goes up by 0.52 points on its six-point Likert-type scale. Knowing these *B* weights, I can create an equation to predict the collaborative competency level of student affairs professionals as follows:

> Collaborative Competency Level = *Constant* (which I can find in a table in my output for my multiple regression) + (3.21 * Terminal Degree) + (2.88 * Senior-Level Position) + (0.52 * Perceptions of an Institutional Collaborative Culture) + error (error indicating that this equation is not going to give me a perfectly accurate prediction but a good one nonetheless)

The *B* weights provide the raw score in terms of the units of measurement that you use. But I cannot really compare a category such as whether someone has a terminal degree to a scaled measure such as institutional collaborative culture. Therefore, I turn to my standardized regression coefficients (my beta weights) to make easy comparisons. These numbers are in standard deviation units for the independent and the dependent variables. For example, increasing the perception of an institutional collaborative culture by one standard deviation (average distance from the average) increases the collaborative competency level by 0.33 standard deviation. Examining beta weights allows me to see that collaborative culture has the strongest influence, followed by terminal degree, and then senior level position (both of which are very close in influence to each other). I hope this example from research helps to illustrate how B weights and beta weights are important and helpful.

Multiple regression is critical to quantitative research. Understanding this section will serve you well. Because there is a lot of information packed into this chapter, I conclude with Table 8.2, a summary of key points on multiple regression.

TABLE 8.2
Multiple Regression Summary Table

Topic	Explanation	Additional Notes
Category of question	Relationship among variables	
Independent variables	Multiple independent variables that attempt to predict the outcome of the dependent variable	The independent variables should be scale variables or categorical (each with only two subcategories coded as 0 or 1).
Dependent variables	Only one dependent variable, and it must be a scale variable	
Statistical significance	The results found in the multiple regression model are likely to be found in the population as well	
Effect size: R^2	The percentage of the variance the combined independent variables in the multiple regression predict for the dependent variable	

(Continues)

TABLE 8.2 *(Continued)*

Topic	Explanation	Additional Notes
Effect size: *B* weights	The unstandardized (raw score in the same units of measurement as the independent variable) measure of the impact of the independent variable	This is the impact of a single independent variable while statistically removing the impact of all other independent variables in the model.
Effect size: *beta* weights	The standardized (always presented in standard deviation units) measure of the impact of the independent variable	This is the impact on the dependent variable (in standard deviation units) when the independent variable increases by one standard deviation (while also statistically removing the impact of all other independent variables in the model).
The gift (what you get)	The results of a multiple regression give you the components of an equation that allow using the independent variables to predict the value of the dependent variable	The accuracy of this equation depends on the R^2 of the multiple regression (how much the model accounts for versus how much is left for error).
Sample size guide	At least your number of independent variables multiplied by 8 plus 50	Another simple rule of thumb is to aim for at least a sample size of 100.

Review Questions From This Chapter

Use the following review questions to test yourself. When you test yourself, you force yourself to recall information, and the act of recalling leads to better and deeper learning.

- What type of question does multiple regression answer?
- What do you get from a multiple regression?

- What do you know about independent and dependent variables in a multiple regression?
- How do you judge effect size in a multiple regression?

Homework

Now that you have a sense of what multiple regression is and does, please search the Internet for the following article and read it:

Soria, K. M., Roberts, J. E., & Reinhard, A. P. (2015). First-year college students' strengths awareness and perceived leadership development. *Journal of Student Affairs Research and Practice*, *52*(1), 89–103.

Soria and colleagues use multiple regression to examine how strengths awareness influences leadership development in almost 800 first-year students. It is a great example of how multiple regression can be a way to do student affairs slow for the betterment of college students.

9

STATISTICAL APPROACH
FOR COMPARING GROUPS

Sharyl is excited about her progress with researching multicultural competence in college students. She read the chapter
on multiple regression three times. Concepts that made her
feel as if she were learning a foreign language now seem familiar.
Some of them just make plain sense. She searched the literature specifically for studies that use multiple regression. Although she once
avoided the methods and results sections of research articles, these
areas are now becoming her favorite. She now searches the results
sections of articles to find the effect size. After developing a scale to
measure multicultural competence, she conducted her own multiple
regression and found the results fascinating. Her confidence in her
ability to be a scholar practitioner is growing, and she feels ready for
a new statistical challenge. Sharyl wants to know how she can use
other statistical approaches to answer their corresponding research
questions. She tackled the question of relationship among variables,
but what about the question of comparing groups?

Overview

I chose to first discuss the quantitative research question category
of relationship among variables and its corresponding statistical
approach, multiple regression, because I think it is the most important as it is the most commonly used. In fact, I could make the
argument that everything you learn from this chapter is simply a

reorganizing of what was in the last chapter. In other words, almost all statistical methods use correlation or regression, just in different ways. Therefore, the differences among the statistical methods presented in this book are more conceptual than technical. I highly recommend reading Chapter 8 multiple times until you feel you have grasped the concepts. Then, learning this chapter will simply entail building on the foundation already laid in your mind from the previous chapter. And that is the best way to learn statistics.

The other three quantitative research question categories are comparing groups, predicting groups, and analyzing structure. In a format similar to the previous chapter on multiple regression, I provide an overview for comparing groups using *t*-tests and ANOVA. I emphasize the most important points and completely leave out less important points to avoid overwhelming you. I discuss statistical significance and effect size, and I conclude with an example from my own research. Figure 9.1 is a reminder of our scaffold of descriptive and inferential statistics.

Figure 9.1. Overview of descriptive and inferential statistics.

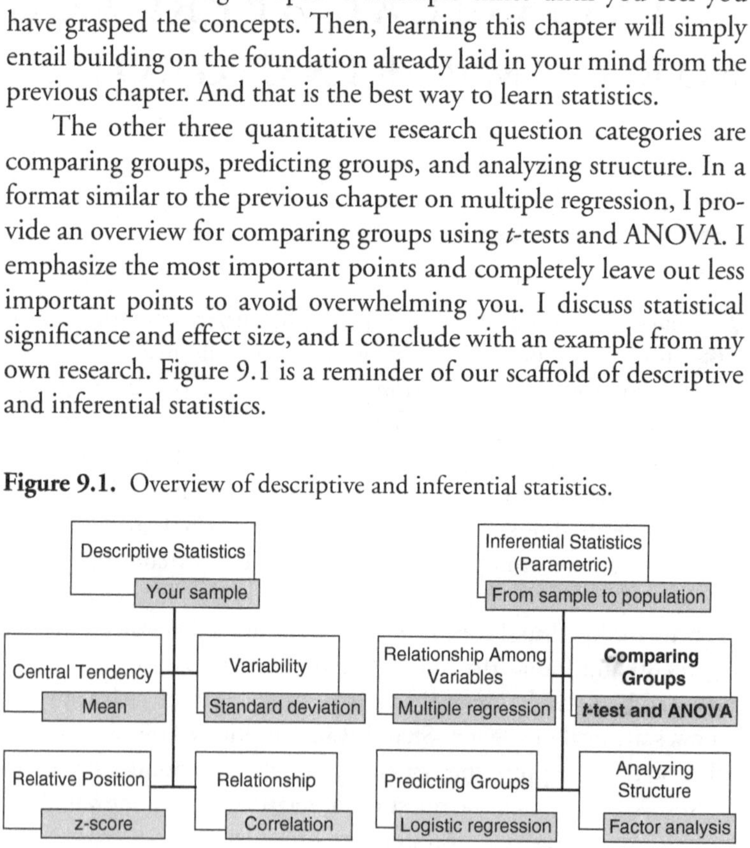

Comparing Groups

Let's go back for a moment to research design. If you recall, I gave you two and a half research designs you need to know: nonexperimental, experimental, and quasi-experimental. Multiple regression, discussed in Chapter 8, is a perfect example of a statistical approach for a nonexperimental research design. In multiple regression, you are studying one group, trying to determine what independent variables significantly and meaningfully predict your one dependent variable. The statistical approaches I discuss in this chapter can be applied to experimental and quasi-experimental designs. These designs compare groups that occur naturally without your intervention (quasi-experimental) or groups that occur because you randomly assigned people to those groups (experimental). When comparing groups, you have three statistical approaches to choose from: a *t*-test, an ANOVA, or more sophisticated versions of ANOVA. Let's tackle each of these.

The t-*test*

A *t*-test is used to determine if a significant difference (and how much of a difference) exists between two groups. Depending on your needs, you can conduct a one-sample *t*-test, an independent samples *t*-test, and a paired (dependent) samples *t*-test. A one-sample *t*-test compares a group to a preselected score. It is rarely used but could be useful, however, in certain situations. For example, if you want to know how a group of students' SAT scores compare to a preselected score, you could use a one-sample *t*-test. Or perhaps you have a GPA cutoff score to determine eligibility for certain student organizations. You can use a one-sample *t*-test to find how a particular group of students as a whole compares to that preselected GPA score.

The two most common uses of the *t*-test, however, are independent samples and paired (dependent) samples. You use an independent samples *t*-test when you compare two separate groups, and you use a paired or dependent samples *t*-test when you make two comparisons within the same group. In other words, a paired or dependent samples *t*-test compares the same group before and after an intervention (see Table 9.1).

TABLE 9.1

Three Types of *t*-Test

Type of *t*-Test	Purpose
One sample	Compares a group to a preselected score
Independent samples	Compares two separate groups (the groups are independent of one another)
Paired (dependent) samples	Compares the same group on two scores

So if you wanted to research multicultural competence, you could do so in two ways. With an independent samples *t*-test, you could compare the multicultural competence of those who go through your multicultural programming to those who do not go through your programming. By contrast, using a paired samples *t*-test, you could compare the multicultural competence of a group of people before they experience your multicultural programming to the multicultural competence of the same group after they experience your programming. So in an independent samples *t*-test, you only measure their multicultural competence once. In a paired samples *t*-test, you measure twice (before and after the intervention, which in this case is your multicultural programming).

From a statistical power perspective, a paired samples *t*-test is much more powerful than an independent samples *t*-test. Why? When you measure the same people twice, you reduce your error compared to measuring two different groups of people. In other words, you can make more direct comparisons when you compare Joe 1 to Joe 2, than when you compare Joe to Dave. This has implications for research design. All other things being equal, plan for a pretest-posttest research design (paired samples). When this is not practical (or not desired from a research perspective), then do a between-groups (independent samples) research design. Although *t*-tests are useful, they are also limited in sophistication. Sometimes you want to compare more than two groups, control for certain variables, or compare groups on more than one dependent variable. When you desire any of these sophistications, you need to advance to ANOVA.

ANOVA

ANOVA is a more sophisticated version of the *t*-test. These sophistications allow you to compare as many groups as you desire, control for any variables, and use multiple dependent variables. Each of these sophistications alters the name of the statistical analysis (so you can tell what is happening just by the name). So what we really have is a MANCOVA, where *M* stands for multivariate, which means more than one dependent variable, and *C* stands for covariate, which is a control variable. Let's break this down further as illustrated in Table 9.2.

TABLE 9.2

Types of ANOVA (Analysis of Variance)

Acronym	Full Name	Purpose	Example	Notes
ANOVA	Analysis of variance	Compares two or more groups on one dependent variable	I want to compare students in three residential communities (independent variable) on the dependent variable of faculty support.	If you only compare two groups, there is no difference between a *t*-test and an ANOVA.
MANOVA	Multivariate analysis of variance	Compares two or more groups on multiple dependent variables	I want to compare students in three residential communities (independent variable) on faculty support (dependent variable 1) and staff support (dependent variable 2).	The dependent variables must intuitively relate to each other. Faculty support and staff support are somewhat related, so I can use both. I could not use faculty support and financial aid, because there is not an intuitive connection between the two variables.
ANCOVA	Analysis of covariance	Compares two or more groups on one dependent variable while controlling for the influence of other variables	I want to compare students in three residential communities (independent variable) on faculty support (dependent variable) while controlling for the influences of college entrance test scores (covariate).	If I believed that high-achieving students may perceive faculty support differently, I can use college entrance test scores as a covariate (control variable) to remove its influence on faculty support.
MANCOVA	Multivariate analysis of covariance	Compares two or more groups on multiple dependent variables while also controlling for the influence of other variables	I want to compare students in three residential communities (independent variable) on faculty support (dependent variable 1) and staff support (dependent variable 2) while controlling for the influences of college entrance test scores (covariate).	This approach combines all the approaches into the most sophisticated version of ANOVA by using multiple dependent variables and control variables.

The information in Table 9.2 is a lot to take in. You may want to refer to this table for the rest of your life. (Feel free to bend the corner of this page as a place marker.) Let me try to address some possible points of confusion. The multivariate version of ANOVA (MANOVA) allows you to compare groups on multiple dependent variables. The way the statistical analysis accomplishes this feat is by combining your multiple dependent variables into one super variable and then comparing your groups with this one super variable. After comparing your groups with this one super variable, it divides the super variable into the original dependent variables and analyzes each one separately. By doing this, you can see not only if there are differences among your groups with the super variable but also the impact of each individual dependent variable. Because a multivariate ANOVA combines the dependent variables into a super variable, these dependent variables must make intuitive sense to combine in the first place. If the dependent variables have nothing to do with each other conceptually, then it is a mistake to combine them.

Another point of confusion can be with the covariate version of ANOVA (ANCOVA). You might remember that in multiple regression, the analysis tells you the influence of each independent variable while removing the influence of (controlling for) the other independent variables. This allows you to see the impact of each independent variable with all other things being equal. This is commonly referred to as a *control variable* because you are controlling for its effects before examining the effects of other variables. In higher education, prior high school achievement (including college entrance scores) is often controlled to analyze the impact of other variables after removing the impact of what was accomplished in high school. This is a very powerful tool.

Variables

Categories of variables when comparing groups are fairly straightforward. The independent variable is always nominal (categorical) because it represents the groups you want to compare. This variable can have as many categories as you like. So if your independent variable is sex, you compare women and men. If your independent variable is classification of year, you compare first-year students, sophomores, juniors, and seniors. In your statistical software, each of these categories must be represented by a number. If you have two categories, I suggest assigning codes to the categories by using 0 and 1 (e.g., woman = 0, man = 1). If you have multiple categories, code in the way that makes the most sense to you (e.g., first-year = 1, sophomore = 2, junior = 3, senior = 4).

Can you have more than one independent variable? Yes. An ANOVA with one independent variable is a one-way ANOVA. An ANOVA with two independent variables is a two-way ANOVA. The general term for multiple independent variables is *factorial ANOVA*. In this case, you could have sex and classification of year as independent variables, resulting in the comparison of first-year women, first-year men, sophomore women, sophomore men, junior women, junior men, senior women, and senior men. This gets complex very quickly. It also requires large sample sizes, as I explain next.

Sample Size for ANOVA

Sample size in ANOVA is more complex than multiple regression because you need to think about the sample size of each individual subcategory, sometimes referred to as cells. When you divide a group, you create more cells. So if you compare women and men, you have two cells. If you compare classifications of year, you have four cells. If you conduct a factorial ANOVA using sex and classification of year, you have eight cells.

The bottom line is that you want a sample size of at least 20 in each cell. When you have two cells, that would mean a sample size of 40, assuming half were women and half were men. In higher education, there is rarely equal representation of sex, so be sure to include as much of your population as possible so that you end up with at least 20 in each cell by the time you are ready to analyze your data. Some of your population will not respond to survey requests. Others will only fill out a small part of the survey, and you will have to exclude them from your data. Sample size can drop quickly, so always err on the side of larger samples. Maintaining at least 20 in each cell for a factorial ANOVA becomes difficult because it means you need 20 first-year women, 20 first-year men, 20 sophomore women, 20 sophomore men, and so on.

Interpreting Results: Statistical Significance

As a reminder, statistical significance has to do with whether differences you find in your sample can also be inferred in your population. When there is a 95% chance or higher of making that inference correctly, you have statistical significance (p is less than or equal to 0.05). Every statistical procedure uses a particular test of significance. In multiple regression, the test of significance is called an F-test, which is also used in an ANOVA because ANOVA and multiple regression are simply different ways of conceptualizing the same statistical analysis. You will find the results of this test in the ANOVA table of results in your statistical output. If the number is less than or equal to 0.05, then the results are considered statistically significant.

But wait. I need to complicate things a bit if you conduct a MANOVA (multivariate ANOVA). ANOVA assumes you are only conducting the test once. In a MANOVA, you conduct several ANOVAs, one for each dependent variable. In other words, the MANOVA compares your groups using the super variable it creates (e.g., combined support from faculty and staff). It then compares groups by each individual dependent variable (e.g., comparing groups on faculty support and then separately comparing groups on staff support). Because you are doing something that is not allowed (conducting multiple ANOVAs), you must compensate by adjusting your significance level. This is referred to as Bonferroni's adjustment (Mertler & Reinhart, 2017). To conduct this adjustment, you start with a maximum p-value of 0.05 (a typical threshold for statistical significance) and divide by the number of dependent variables. In my example, I have two dependent variables: faculty support and staff support. So I conduct Bonferroni's adjustment to get a new threshold of significance of 0.025 ($0.05 \div 2 = 0.025$). This means that for my multivariate dependent variable (combined faculty and staff support), I will use 0.05 as the cutoff for statistical significance. But for my individual ANOVAs that compare faculty support and staff support separately, I will not consider my results to be statistically significant unless the p-value is less than or equal to 0.025.

When it comes to statistical significance for the question of comparing groups, you are ultimately asking whether differences found among the groups can also be inferred in your population.

This is a yes or no question. The next and more important question is, How much of a difference is there among my groups? That brings us to effect size.

Interpreting Results: Effect Size

Conceptually, effect size in ANOVA is the same as effect size in multiple regression. In multiple regression, effect size is calculated by R^2, which represents the proportion (percentage) of variance the independent variables explain for the dependent variable. An R^2 of 0.28 in a multiple regression means that the combination of independent variables explains 28% of the variance in the dependent variable.

ANOVA works the same way but with different names. Most often, effect size in ANOVA is determined by eta squared (η^2). Variations of ANOVA might use a calculation with a different name, such as omega squared (Ω^2). No matter which specific calculation and name is used, the result is interpreted the same way as r^2. Therefore, an η^2 of 0.28 in an ANOVA means that the independent variable (the group the participant is in) explains 28% of the variance in your dependent variable. Continuing with my example, it might mean that classification of year explains 28% of the variance in faculty support. I could then compare the averages of each group (first-year, sophomore, junior, senior) to determine which group has more faculty support than another. Effect size tells me how much of a difference can be attributed to classification of year. If you desire a simple rule of thumb for categorizing the relative size of an effect in ANOVA, I recommend the following:

(same as r^2)

- ~~0.01~~ = small effect size .06   6%
- ~~0.10~~ = medium effect size . 12   12%
- ~~0.20~~ = large effect size . 20   20%

This means that when the difference in groups explains 20% or more of the effect in your dependent variable, you have a large impact. But again, this is a rule of thumb that does not take into account the makeup of your groups or your specific dependent variable. So intuition (thinking fast) may lead you to make discernments on the size of the effect that differ from this general guideline.

The Gift of ANOVA

If you recall, the gift of multiple regression is that it provides you with a formula for predicting a dependent variable based on two or more independent variables. ANOVA does not provide you with such a formula. What it does provide, however, is the direct influence that particular groupings have on one or more dependent variables that interest you. One thing I hope readers take away from this book is that I want to encourage student affairs professionals to conduct more experiments. ANOVA is a statistical approach for comparing groups in a way that directly connects to your experimental (or quasi-experimental) design. So much of the historic research on college students is based on White males. ANOVA allows us to determine conditional effects, or the effects that sex or race may have on an outcome.

ANOVA in Use

For ANOVA, my example is a study I did for my dissertation, which was published in the *Journal of College Student Retention* (Sriram, 2014b). Because I noticed that experimental designs are common in fields such as psychology but rare in the higher education literature, I wanted to conduct an experimental design for my dissertation. I was inspired by Dweck's (2006) work on mind-set, namely the theories we have about ourselves and how those theories shape our behaviors. In particular, I was interested in mind-set concerning intelligence. In this context, a growth mind-set is the belief that intelligence can be developed, whereas a fixed mind-set represents the belief that intelligence is innate and unchangeable. I was concerned about academically high-risk students in remedial programs and wanted to know three things. First, could I foster a growth mind-set for intelligence in academically high-risk students? Second, would a growth mind-set make a difference in the amount of effort they put forth in their academic experiences? Third, would a growth mind-set make a difference in academic achievement?

The abstract of my article reads, "This study utilized an experimental pretest-posttest control group design" (Sriram, 2014b, p. 515). Look at me trying to sound smart! These kinds of statements should now make sense to you, especially as you break them down into chunks. The first chunk is the word *experimental*. This means that I compared groups, and I randomly assigned people to these groups. If I had not used random assignment, I would have used the term *quasi-experimental*. The second chunk is *pretest-posttest*. This means that I measured these groups before my treatment (pretest) and then measured them again after my treatment (posttest). The third chunk is *control group*, meaning I compared my treatment group to a group that had a similar experience without the treatment.

All the students in my study were required to take a remedial course on study skills and other tips for academic success. Working with the department in charge of academic support programs, I randomly assigned academically high-risk, first-year students to one of two groups. The first group was my treatment group, which took part in an online intervention consisting of four 15-minute sessions in which I tried to teach the group to have a growth mind-set of intelligence. The second group was my control group, which participated in four 15-minute online sessions in which I tried to teach study skills. I made sure that both groups participated in online sessions so that any differences I found could be attributed to the content of the sessions rather than the fact that one group was getting more attention than another. I taught study skills in my control group because that is what the students were already learning in the remedial course. Therefore, I was comparing the new content on growth mind-set to the current content of study skills taught in the remedial course.

I compared groups twice in my research study, using *t*-tests and ANOVA. I wanted to know whether I could encourage academically high-risk students to have a growth mind-set of intelligence. To think slow about this question, I conducted a paired samples *t*-test. Remember, a paired samples *t*-test compares a group to itself (before and after an intervention). In fact, I conducted two paired samples *t*-tests, one for the mind-set (treatment) group and one for the study skills (control) group. I found that the treatment group changed to a more growth mind-set, and this change had a large effect size. I measured effect size with Cohen's *d* (discussed in Chapter 7). Cohen's *d* calculates effect size in terms of standard deviation. The effect size for my mind-set (treatment) group was 0.81. This represents a large effect (see Table 7.8 on how to interpret Cohen's d). For my study skills (control) group, there was no difference in their mind-set of intelligence before and after their study skills intervention (which is what I would have expected).

Thanks to my paired samples t-tests, I knew that my intervention worked in encouraging more of a growth mind-set in my treatment group. I also learned that the mind-set of my control group did not change. Now came the question of whether the growth mind-set of intelligence group (independent variable based on group) was different in academic effort (dependent variable) from the study skills group. To answer this question, I conducted a MANCOVA. The M means that I had multiple dependent variables to measure academic effort, and the C means that I also had at least one control variable. The multiple dependent variables consisted of six scales that measured six latent variables that I thought related to academic effort: academic discipline, academic self-confidence, commitment to college, general determination, goal striving, and study skills. Because I measured my participants on all these variables before and after my experiment, I could use all six pretest scores as covariates. This means that I could determine if there was a difference in these six variables after accounting for where each individual started with each of these six variables. Therefore, I was comparing each group to itself (pretest and posttest) and comparing the two groups to each other (mind-set group versus study skills group). So I was basically using a paired samples t-test within an ANOVA. That's the beauty of using covariates in an ANOVA.

A MANCOVA takes your related dependent variables and combines them into a super variable before comparing groups. The results showed me that the two groups differed significantly on the multivariate variable (super variable) of academic effort. Statistical significance means that I could infer the results from my sample to my population (all first-year, high risk students at that institution). My effect size (partial η^2) was .213. This means that 21.3% of the variance in academic effort could be attributed to whether the students were in the mind-set intervention or the study skills control group. In other words, the mind-set intervention had a large impact on their academic effort.

It gets even cooler. After comparing groups on my super variable of academic effort, the analysis compared groups on each individual dependent variable that made up academic effort (academic discipline, academic self-confidence, commitment to college, general determination, goal striving, and study skills). Each one of those latent variables represented a scale in the survey I administered at the beginning and end of my study. When I compared the mind-set group to the study skills group on each of these six variables, only study skills was statistically significant (I used Bonferroni's adjustment). It was also the only variable with a medium effect size (partial $\eta^2 = 0.13$).

Do you see the irony here? My experiment demonstrated that teaching academically high-risk students a growth mind-set of intelligence caused them to employ more study skills than the group to which I taught more study skills. How interesting is that?! I love research. I interpreted my findings by theorizing that the growth mind-set removed psychological barriers to change that caused those students in the growth mind-set group to actually employ the study skills they were taught in the remedial course.

I did not, however, find a meaningful difference between the two groups on academic achievement (as measured by end-of-semester GPA). I have theories for why that was the case, but you will need to read Sriram (2014b) if you are interested to know what they are. Table 9.3 provides a summary of ANOVA.

TABLE 9.3
ANOVA Summary Table

Topic	Explanation	Additional Notes
Type of question	**Comparing groups**	
Independent variables	Independent variables represent your groupings. For example, one independent variable might be race.	The independent variables are nominal (categorical) because they represent different groups.
Dependent variables	Dependent variables must be scale variables (measured on a continuum).	

(Continues)

TABLE 9.3 (*Continued*)

Topic	Explanation	Additional Notes
Type of question	Comparing groups	
Statistical significance	Statistical significance means that differences found among groups in your sample can also be inferred in the population.	
Effect size: partial η^2	This is the percentage of the variance in the dependent variable explained by the group (independent variable).	
The gift (what you get)	Comparing groups is simple to understand and easy to communicate.	
Sample size guide	You should end up with at least a sample size of 20 in each cell (grouping).	

Review Questions From This Chapter

Use the following review questions to test yourself. When you test yourself, you force yourself to recall information, and the act of recalling leads to better and deeper learning.

- What type of question does ANOVA answer?
- What are the different types of ANOVA, and what do they accomplish (e.g., MANOVA)?
- What do you know about independent and dependent variables in an ANOVA?
- How do you judge effect size in an ANOVA?

Homework

Now that you have a sense of what ANOVA is and does, please search the Internet for the following article and read it:

Johnson, D. R., Soldner, M., Leonard, J. B., Alvarez, P., Inke-las, K. K., Rowan-Kenyon, H. T., & Longerbeam, S. D. (2007). Examining sense of belonging among first-year undergraduates from different racial/ethnic groups. *Journal of College Student Development, 48*(5), 525–542.

Johnson and colleagues use ANOVA to examine the sense of belonging in almost 3,000 first-year students—a great example of how ANOVA can be a way to do student affairs slow for the betterment of college students.

10

STATISTICAL APPROACH FOR PREDICTING GROUPS

L eia works in a residential college that aims to bring synergy to the academic and community lives of students. An important aspect of her residential college is that it welcomes students of all classifications of year (first-years, sophomores, juniors, and seniors). It also encourages students to stay in the residential college all four years of their college experience. Some students stay, and some students leave. Leia wants to know why. Specifically, she wants to know what variables in students could help her predict who will want to stay in the residential college and who will not. If Leia could predict which group students will fall into (the stayers or the leavers), she could then think about how to influence those variables that encourage students to stay.

Overview

This chapter addresses the third research question category: predicting groups. The statistical approach for predicting groups is logistic regression. It is not as common as multiple regression or ANOVA, but there are instances in higher education in which logistic regression might be the most helpful approach. I want you to have logistic regression as a statistical tool. Figure 10.1 is a reminder of our statistics scaffold.

Figure 10.1. Overview of descriptive and inferential statistics.

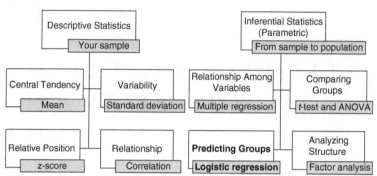

Logistic Regression

Multiple regression, ANOVA, logistic regression, and factor analysis are all tweaked versions of the same idea. Statistics professors treat them as completely different approaches because they are easier to understand and learn that way. But they are all based on regression. The differences lie in what is being regressed to what. So let's review.

Regression is basically another word for correlation (technically, regressions are correlations in which you try to predict one variable from another). Correlation (corelationship) places the relationship among variables on a scale from −1.0 to +1.0. In multiple regression, you determine how two or more independent variables relate to one scale (measured on a continuum) dependent variable. In ANOVA you determine how variables within a group relate to those same variables within another group, causing a direct comparison. In logistic regression, you determine how two or more independent variables relate to one nominal (categorical) dependent variable. The basic purpose of logistic regression is to classify individuals by group, especially so you can make future predictions about which group individuals will fall into.

Variables

Logistic regression seeks to identify a combination of independent variables that best predicts membership in a particular group, as measured by a nominal (categorical) dependent variable. Simply put, logistic regression is the same as multiple regression, but the dependent variable now only has categories (instead of being measured on a continuum as in multiple regression). Typically, the dependent variable in logistic regression only has two categories, which is known as a binary logistic regression. A more sophisticated version—multinomial logistic regression—allows three or more categories in the dependent variable.

Independent variables in logistic regression follow the same rules as multiple regression. The independent variables should typically be measured on a continuum (scale variables). However, you can use *dummy coding*, which consists of taking a two-category variable and coding it using a 0 and a 1, for logistic regression as you do in multiple regression. This trick allows you to use scale variables and two-category nominal variables for your independent variables.

A big advantage of logistic regression is that you can dump independent variables into the analysis with little worry of hurting the analysis. If you have a slight theoretical reason for including a variable, include it.

Three Approaches of Logistic Regression

The three primary ways of conducting a logistic regression are standard, hierarchical, and stepwise. These three versions are the same three approaches for multiple regression (discussed in Chapter 8, p. 137). With standard logistic regression, you enter all independent variables into the calculations at the same time, thereby allowing the software to address them all together to see what you get. When you want to control the order in which the independent variables are entered into the calculations, you conduct a hierarchical logistic regression. In this approach, the independent variables believed to be most influential are entered first, and subsequent independent variables are added to determine the specific amount of variance they each may add. Stepwise logistic regression allows the software to determine the order that the independent variables are entered into the calculations.

Sample Size

In similar fashion to multiple regression, problems occur in logistic regression if there are too few cases relative to the number of independent variables. With multiple regression, I suggested a sample size of 100 to reach a threshold of performing well statistically. I am keeping that recommendation for logistic regression. The more independent variables you have, however, the greater the sample size required. A sample size of 100 should work well for you in most cases, but if you have a high number of independent variables (approaching 10 or more), then 100 may not be enough.

Sample size is not the only factor to consider in logistic regression, however. Because you attempt to predict groups, it is important to have enough participants fall into each of the groups of your dependent variable. Remember, this approach makes future predictions from past data. Therefore, the logistic regression needs balanced information to make accurate predictions. If you have two groups, you ideally want 50% of your sample to fall into each of your two groups. This ideal situation will probably not happen in your research, but if your sample gets more lopsided than a 70/30 split, it may hurt your results.

Interpreting Results: Statistical Significance

By now, *statistical significance* should be familiar to you, and you should be able to define it in your own words. Statistical significance should also feel somewhat uninteresting. After all, it does not tell you that much information, and others make a much bigger deal of statistical significance than it warrants. Statistical significance tells you if you can make inferences in your population from your sample (with 95% confidence).

The output of a logistic regression provides you with four primary tables: one for the overall logistic regression model (model summary table), one for each step of the model (step summary table), one called a classification table, and one called a table of coefficients. The step summary table will have a column titled *Sig.* (significance). This column represents the *p*-values. If the *p*-value is less than 0.05, you have statistical significance for the model.

Interpreting Results: Effect Size

Probability and odds. There is a lot to interpret regarding effect size in a logistic regression. Logistic regression attempts to predict the probability that one of the categories of the dependent variable will occur. Two important terms to learn are *probability* and *odds*. Probability is a value predicted by logistic regression that ranges from 0 to 1. If you roll a die, what is the probability you will roll a six? There are six possibilities on a die, and there is only one 6. Therefore, the probability is 1/6, or 0.167. Likewise, the probability of flipping a coin and getting heads is 1/2, or 0.5. The probability will always be between 0 and 1.

Except in Las Vegas, odds are not commonly used. The odds are calculated by taking the probability for something occurring and dividing it by the probability of it not occurring (Mertler & Reinhart, 2017). So the odds of rolling a six equals the probability of rolling a six (0.167) divided by the probability of not rolling a six $(1 - 0.167 = 0.833)$. The result of $0.167 \div 0.833$ is 2. So the odds of rolling a six equals 2. The odds of getting heads when you flip a coin equals 1 $(0.5 \div 0.5 = 1)$. If you have 100 ping-pong balls in a large jar labeled with numbers from 1 to 100, the probability of pulling out the number 37 is 0.01 $(1 \div 100 = 0.01)$. The odds are also 0.01 $(0.01 \div 0.99 = 0.01)$. When it comes to odds, think of the number 1 as the tipping point. Anything above 1 puts odds in favor of an event occurring. Anything below 1 means odds are not in favor of an event occurring. Odds of 1 means there is a 50/50 chance of an event occurring.

The purpose of this book is not to bombard you with math, and you might feel that I am getting too math heavy here. I need to explain probability and odds because this is the language used by logistic regression. You should understand that an odds ratio greater than 1 shows a positive relationship between the independent and dependent variables (when the independent variable increases, the chances of falling into a certain category also increases). An odds ratio less than 1 indicates a negative relationship (when the independent variable increases, the chances of falling into a certain category decreases). When you use or encounter logistic regression, you can come back to this section to help you interpret the results.

Cox & Snell's R^2 *and Nagelgerke's* R^2. One way that logistic regression provides you an effect size is with R^2. Like multiple regression, this calculation represents the proportion of the dependent variable that can be explained by your combination of independent variables. Therefore, it represents the effect size of the logistic regression as a whole.

There are two methods for calculating R^2. The difference is that the Cox & Snell R^2 is a more conservative calculation, meaning that it will almost always be smaller than the Nagelgerke R^2. It is common to report both. So if the Nagelgerke R^2 is 0.79, that means that the independent variables in your logistic regression explain 79% of the variance of group membership (your dependent variable).

Classification or percentage correct. The classification table is pretty neat. It tells you, based on the software's calculations, what group it would have predicted each individual to fall into. It then compares this prediction to the groups the individuals were actually in and therefore provides you with the percentage of cases for which the model accurately predicted the correct group. If you were to make such predictions by thinking fast, you would have a 50/50 shot at getting it right. So if the percentage of cases that the logistic regression model accurately predicted is more than 50%, you know that the model is better than chance and is actually helpful. Knowing this percentage tells you exactly how helpful.

Table of coefficients or variables in the equation (B weights and Exp[B]). So far, we have only thought about the performance of the logistic regression as a whole model. What about the individual independent variables? This is where the table of coefficients comes into play. There are two measures of effect I want you to know: *B* weights and *Exp(B)*.

You may remember *B* weights from multiple regression. This is an unstandardized score, meaning that it is presented in the same units that the independent variable was measured. In essence, the *B* weight represents the change in the odds of predicting the dependent variable (group membership) when the independent variable increases by one unit. *B* weights are most important for how they lead to the calculation of *Exp(B)*.

Exp(B) is what you really want to know about your independent variables in a logistic regression. *Exp(B)* represents the odds ratio. It is the change in odds when your independent variable increases by one unit. This allows you to quickly compare which independent variables have the greatest impact on the prediction of group membership. An odds ratio greater than 1 shows a positive relationship between the independent and dependent variables, whereas an odds ratio less than 1 indicates a negative predictive relationship. The closer to 1, the smaller the effect.

Some authors discuss the use of another form of effect size in logistic regression, called delta-*p* (Cruce, 2009; Mayhew et al., 2016; Peng & So, 2002). I do not discuss it here, but you should read those works if you are interested in learning more about it.

Simplifying for sanity. I sympathize that there is a lot to interpret for logistic regression. Let me simplify this for you. First, you want to look at R^2 and determine how much of the variance in groups is predicted by your combined independent variables. Second, you want to examine the percentage correctly so that you can see how accurate the model is in its predictions. Third, you want to look at *Exp(B)* to get a comparative sense of which independent variables are the most influential in predicting group membership.

The Gift of Logistic Regression

The question of what causes people to land in one group as opposed to another is a helpful one to ask and an interesting one to answer. This is the gift of logistic regression. You might think that having a two-group dependent variable is a rare occurrence. Besides retention, variables rarely divide themselves into just two groups. The good news is that you can create two groups with nearly any variable. For example, if you have a scale that measures a latent variable of interest to you (e.g., my example of faculty support), you can divide respondents into two categories: those who have a faculty support score above the average and those who have a score below the average. This new two-category variable (low faculty support versus high faculty support) can be used as your dependent variable in logistic regression. If you need to use a dependent variable with more than two groups, you can use the more sophisticated multinomial logistic regression, which is the method used in the following example from published research.

Logistic Regression in Use

I have never used logistic regression in my research. Therefore, to describe logistic regression in use, I draw from Bentley-Edwards, Agonafer, Edmondson, and Flannigan's (2016) article on racial factors and goal efficacy. They studied 242 Black college students to understand what variables influence their goal efficacy, people's own appraisal that they can achieve their goals. When someone's preferred goal matches her or his expected outcome, that person has goal efficacy. Their research question was, Do racial factors influence goal efficacy?

To answer this question, Bentley-Edwards and colleagues (2016) used a series of scales that measured racial cohesion (16 items, α = 0.82), Black racial dissonance (seven items, α = 0.71), cultural racism (10 items, α = 0.78), institutional racism (six items, α = 0.69), and individual racism (six items, α = 0.78). As a reminder, α refers to Cronbach's alpha, which is the most common way to measure reliability. My recommended threshold for a reliable scale is 0.70, so I would judge all these scales as reasonably accurate measures of their respective latent variables.

Bentley-Edwards and colleagues (2016) used a multinomial logistic regression in their search for truth. Their independent variables were racial cohesion, racial agency, racial dissonance, cultural racism, institutional racism, and individual racism. Their dependent variable related to participants' goals. Goals were categorized into five groups: professional career, skilled career, entertainment/sports, lifestyle, and unsure.

Could their independent variables be used to predict the category of goals of Black college students? Here's what they found. Black college students in their sample who reported high individual racism stress were more likely to report being unsure of their goals. High cultural racism positively predicted choosing a lifestyle goal over a professional career goal. Students who were low in racial agency were more likely to choose entertainment/sports over a career goal. Lower racial agency was also related to being unsure of their goals. A high sense of cohesion predicted choosing a lifestyle goal or an entertainment/sports goal. And racial dissonance did not predict any goal categories (Bentley-Edwards et al., 2016). All the odds ratios were small (just above or below 1), so it is important to note that these effects were rather small.

This summary of the work of Bentley-Edwards and colleagues (2016) does not fully do the article justice. There is much more to their work, which they report in their article, and I recommend you read it. I appreciate this article not only for its content, the truth they search for, but also for the clever way they conceptualize their data to use logistic regression. They conceptualized different goals as different groupings, and they used logistic regression to predict those groupings. Table 10.1 provides a summary of logistic regression.

TABLE 10.1

Logistic Regression Summary Table

Topic	Explanation	Additional Notes
Type of question	Predicting groups	As opposed to relationship among variables, comparing groups, and analyzing structure.
Independent variables	Multiple independent variables that attempt to predict the outcome of the dependent variable	The independent variables should be scale variables or categorical (with only two subcategories coded as 0 or 1).
Dependent variables	Only one dependent variable, and it must be a nominal (categorical) variable	Binary logistic regression has two subcategories; multinomial logistic regression has more than two.
Statistical significance	Statistical significance means that the predictions of the logistic regression model as a whole can be inferred in the population of interest	
Effect size: Cox & Snell R^2/ Nagelkerke R^2	The percentage of the variance that the independent variables in the logistic regression predict for the dependent variable	Cox & Snell is a more conservative calculation, meaning that it will almost always be smaller than Nagelkerke. Report both.
Effect size: Classification/ Percentage correct	A table that tells you how often (in terms of percentages) the model predicts the correct group for your participants	

(Continues)

TABLE 10.1 (*Continued*)

Topic	Explanation	Additional Notes
Effect size: *B* weights	The unstandardized (raw score that is in the same units of measurement as the independent variable) measure of the impact of the independent variable	This is the impact of a single independent variable while statistically removing the impact of all other independent variables in the model.
Effect size: *Exp(B)*	The standardized (always presented in terms of an odds ratio) measure of the impact of the independent variable	This is the impact of a single independent variable while statistically removing the impact of all other independent variables in the model. An odds ratio greater than 1 means that the independent variable positively predicts membership in a particular group.
The gift (what you get)	Thinking in terms of groups can sometimes be more helpful than thinking in terms of measurement on a continuous scale. Therefore, logistic regression allows you to take your scale data and convert it into groups (e.g., satisfied versus unsatisfied students). It then tells you what leads to one group (satisfied) versus the other (unsatisfied).	
Sample size guide	Aim for at least a sample size of 100	With logistic regression, you also need to make sure that enough of your sample falls into each possible group (so that the software has enough information to make predictions).

Review Questions From This Chapter

Use the following review questions to test yourself. When you test yourself, you force yourself to recall information, and the act of recalling leads to better and deeper learning.

- What type of question does logistic regression answer?
- What do you know about independent and dependent variables in a logistic regression?
- How do you judge effect size in a logistic regression?

Homework

Now that you have a sense of what logistic regression is and does, please search the Internet for the following article, in addition to Bentley-Edwards and colleagues (2016), and read it.

Bingham, M. A., & Solverson, N. W. (2016). Using enrollment data to predict retention rate. *Journal of Student Affairs Research and Practice*, 53(1), 51–64.

Bingham and Solverson (2016) use logistic regression to determine the extent to which multiyear, multi-institutional data can predict retention rates at a public university. It is a great example of how logistic regression can be a way to do student affairs slow for the betterment of college students.

STATISTICAL APPROACH
FOR ANALYZING
STRUCTURE

Terri has become comfortable with developing scales and using them in research. She is now more interested in testing ideas as well as testing variables. She wants to capture the bigger picture behind her data. For example, she wants to test whether her latent variables have construct validity. She also has theories for how some latent variables might influence other variables. Terri is ready to examine the underlying patterns in her data. She is ready to analyze structure.

Overview

The last research question category pertains to the underlying structure of variables, how they relate to each other behind the scenes. Use of the research question category is becoming fairly common because of advancements in statistical software. But it is also the most complex. The main reason for the complexity is that it takes regression analysis (e.g., what is done in multiple regression) to the max. The statistical approach for analyzing the underlying structure of variables is called factor analysis. Some versions of factor analysis are difficult to do. However, I think you can conceptually understand in a short time all versions of factor analysis, and that is one of my goals for you in this chapter. Figure 11.1 is a reminder of our

Figure 11.1. Overview of descriptive and inferential statistics.

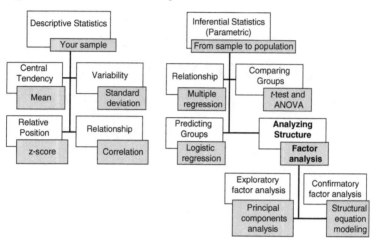

statistics scaffold, with a breakdown of the two approaches for factor analysis.

The Final Research Question Category: Analyzing Structure

Congratulations! You have reached the last of the four quantitative research question categories. What a journey this has been! I presented the four research question categories in the order that I thought would be most useful to you right now (from most useful to least useful). That means, I think the question of analyzing structure is the least useful. Sort of. For me personally, I find the research question category of analyzing structure the most useful. But I may be in a different place than you are. So what you find most useful now may be different from what you find most useful five years from now.

The question of analyzing structure can be paraphrased as, What is going on here? Another related question is, What are the underlying patterns in my data? To address the question of analyzing structure, we use factor analysis.

What is a factor? The good news is that you already know the answer to that question. A factor is a latent variable. Another term we use for latent variable is *component*. So instead of factor analysis, we could call it latent variable analysis or component analysis. Why don't we? If those in statistics called everything that was the same by the same name, it would make it easier for you to learn, which would mean that more people would learn it, which could possibly create job insecurity for statisticians. Therefore, they create multiple names for every term so that you will give up and leave their discipline alone. So if you hear latent variable, factor, or component, think *latent variable*.

Factor analysis searches for truth regarding latent variables. It takes variables and combines them into larger variables. Factor analysis can also determine relationships among all these larger variables, allowing the researcher to develop and confirm a model for how variables interact. If that is a lot to take in, do not feel anxious. Just keep reading.

Two Approaches

There are two primary approaches to factor analysis: exploratory factor analysis and confirmatory factor analysis. If you understand the differences between these two approaches conceptually, you are in really good shape as a scholar practitioner. Let's discuss each of these two approaches and also go through an example of how each might be used in practice.

Exploratory factor analysis. This approach contains the word *explore* because it is a method for searching for underlying patterns in data. When it detects that particular variables relate to one another to strong degrees, it suggests combining those variables into a larger super variable—a latent variable. In other words, exploratory factor analysis is the statistical approach to what you have already done when you developed a scale to measure a latent variable. Ha! Fooled you! You have already done this technique in your head—thinking fast.

Let me explain. Back in Chapter 6, you decided that you wanted to measure a particular latent variable. You then created multiple items in a scale to indirectly measure that latent variable. Therefore, this latent variable of yours is really a super variable (larger combined variable) of all your items (subvariables). It represents the combination of your items in a helpful manner. But how do you know that you were right and justified in claiming that those items really do measure the latent variable? We discussed two concepts: reliability and validity. Reliability is accuracy, measured by Cronbach's alpha. For validity, we discussed the Four Cs: content, criterion related, construct, and conclusion. Exploratory factor analysis is the statistical approach for construct validity. Using statistics, it will tell you if your items really do go together the way you hope they do.

Time for an example. In 2010 ACPA and NASPA jointly published their first list of 10 competencies that all student affairs professionals should possess. This was a milestone for the field of student affairs. The list even included detailed descriptions of what basic, intermediate, and advanced competence should look like. I wanted to know if these competencies could be measured. So I created a series of scales, one scale for each competency, to measure these competencies (Sriram, 2014a). I developed items (subvariables) to measure each competency (latent variable). But how could I really know that one competency was truly a latent variable separate from another competency? In other words, how did I know that *advising and helping* was truly different from *student learning and development*?

To answer this question, and determine construct validity, I conducted an exploratory factor analysis. The method I used, *principal components analysis*, analyzed the underlying patterns of the data (the responses to my items) and gave me feedback on how the item responses grouped together. In other words, the software told me what it thought were my latent variables. When items that I thought measured the latent variable of *student learning and development* were also determined by the exploratory factor analysis to be grouped together, I knew I was on to something. The bottom line is that exploratory factor analysis uses statistics to help determine (validate) the latent variables in your data.

Confirmatory factor analysis. If exploratory factor analysis statistically determines your latent variables, what does confirmatory factor analysis do? Modeling. Scholars like to develop models on how variables fit together. For example, scholars are interested in what leads to college student retention, but there is no simple answer to that question. Therefore, scholars like Braxton, Doyle, Hartley, Hirschy, Jones, and McLendon, (2014) developed models based on lots of data to determine how variables influence each other, allowing them to test theories and make claims. One theory Braxton and colleagues validated was that social integration and academic integration influence students' commitment to the institution, which thereby positively influences retention.

Herein lies an important difference. In exploratory factor analysis, the software tells you what the latent variables are (you are exploring the patterns in your data). In confirmatory factor analysis, you tell the software what your model is, and it either confirms or invalidates your model based on what it finds in the data. Figure 11.2 contains a crude model of my paraphrase of Braxton and colleagues' (2014) work.

Figure 11.2. Part of Braxton and colleagues' retention model.

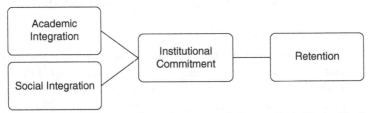

Note. Adapted from *Rethinking College Student Retention*, by Braxton, Doyle, Hartley, Hirschy, Jones, and McLendon, 2014, San Francisco, CA: Jossey-Bass.

Going back to my example on student affairs competencies, I could use exploratory factor analysis (principal components analysis) to determine what latent variables (competencies) exist in my data on student affairs professionals from around the nation. If I gathered a new round of data from student affairs professionals, I could then use confirmatory factor analysis (often referred to as *structural equation modeling*) with this second round of new data to create a model for how competencies might influence each other. Exploratory factor analysis is used in the development of a measurement; confirmatory factor analysis is used to confirm a model or theory (a way of explaining things).

Sample Size

I could easily spend a great deal of time discussing appropriate sample size for factor analysis. Instead, I will be short and to the point. Factor analysis requires lots of data. As a general rule of thumb, I suggest a sample size of 300 for conducting factor analysis. It is certainly possible to get away with a smaller sample (even as low as 150). If you do not have a sample of 300 and still want to conduct factor analysis, a book on principal components analysis or structural equation modeling can explain how to test your data to see if your sample size will work.

Interpreting Results: Exploratory Factor Analysis (Principal Components Analysis)

Interpreting results in factor analysis is conceptualized differently from the other approaches I have discussed. A common statistical approach for conducting exploratory factor analysis is called principal components analysis, a method that can be used with IBM SPSS software.

Principal components analysis deals with an important trade-off. You want to take your items and group them into latent variables (components). This, in a sense, simplifies your data. Instead of thinking about 80 items in your survey, you can now think about 10 latent variables in your survey. But remember the following: When you choose to simplify, you also choose to ignore information. Simplicity involves less truth but is easier to understand. Complexity contains more truth but is harder to understand and use. Therefore, the results of principal components analysis are interpreted based on how much of the original information your new latent variables capture.

If your survey has 80 items, you could have a maximum of 80 latent variables (if each item truly measured something completely different). You could also have a minimum of one latent variable (if all 80 of your items happened to measure the exact same latent variable). How do you decide between those two extremes? Judgments are made regarding how many latent variables to keep using three methods: eigenvalues, scree plots, and total variance explained.

Eigenvalues are a way to measure how much information each latent variable explains. They are based on correlations, which are often referred to as *factor loadings* in factor analysis. A rule of thumb, referred to as Kaiser's rule, suggests that you keep the latent variables that have eigenvalues greater than 1 (because this means that the latent variable explains more than a single item on its own could explain). If you have 80 items in your survey, you might have 15 latent variables with eigenvalues greater than 1. Before you decide to keep 15 latent variables, you need to look at the scree plots.

Scree plots are graphical displays of your latent variables in accordance with how much each latent variable explains. An example of a scree plot is shown in Figure 11.3.

Figure 11.3. Example of a scree plot.

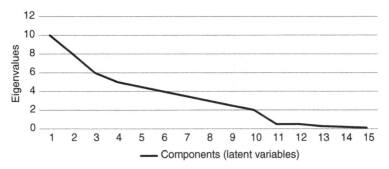

Do you see where the line begins to shift from flat to upward at component 11? This is referred to as the *elbow*. A method for determining how many latent variables to keep is to take those latent variables that occur before the elbow. That means that according to the scree plot you should keep 10 latent variables.

The last way to make judgments regarding your latent variables is to refer to the *total variance explained*. Your statistical output will tell you how much of the total variance each latent variable explains (or accounts for). It will also give you a running total. When that running total reaches 70%, keep just those latent variables that account for that 70%. In other words, a suggested balance between simplicity and complexity is to simplify your data to 70% of all the information available.

Using eigenvalues, scree plots, and total variance explained, along with your intuition and what makes sense to you, is the best way to artfully decide how many latent variables are worth retaining from your exploratory factor analysis. It is important to note that you are not only left with how many latent variables to retain but you also have measures for the relative strength of each latent variable.

Interpreting Results: Confirmatory Factor Analysis (Structural Equation Modeling)

I feel I am giving you more than you bargained for regarding factor analysis. Therefore, I will be extra brief when it comes to interpreting results for confirmatory factor analysis. The statistical method for conducting confirmatory factor analysis is called *structural equation modeling* (because you are building and confirming a model based on your data). Statisticians have developed several different calculations to determine how well your model fits the data. Two of the most common measures are the CFI (confirmatory fit index) and the RMSEA (root mean square error of approximation).

The results of structural equation modeling do not give you a yes or no answer to model fit. Rather, they tell you to what extent your model fits the data (Byrne, 2010). For CFI, a general rule of thumb is the higher, the better.

- Great fit: > 0.95
- Good fit: > 0.93
- Okay fit: > 0.90
- Marginal fit: < 0.89
- Bad fit: < 0.80

For the RMSEA, a general guideline is the lower, the better.

- Great fit: near 0.05
- Mediocre fit: > 0.08
- Bad fit: > 0.10

The Gift of Factor Analysis

Factor analysis provides you with the big picture of your data. Whether you are validating a scale you developed or validating a model you created, factor analysis provides a beautiful blend of theory and statistical evidence. Both forms of factor analysis allow you to determine the relationships among a multitude of variables. Both allow you to get a better understanding of the latent variables in your data. Exploratory factor analysis uses relationships among variables to unveil the latent variables in your survey. Confirmatory factor analysis uses relationships to determine how latent variables influence each other.

Factor Analysis in Use

As someone who has served as a faculty in residence in a residential college, student-faculty relationships are important and fascinating to me. A graduate student of mine, Melissa McLevain, worked in the residential college with me, and we would often discuss the types of relationships that faculty in residence have with students. We wanted to know how we could measure those relationships.

Melissa and I decided (Sriram & McLevain, 2016) to develop a scale—more specifically, a series of scales—to measure student-faculty interactions for faculty in residence in residential colleges. We organized student-faculty interaction into three distinct categories of engagement: academic, social, and deeper life interactions. We defined *deeper life interactions* as those that occur regarding life's big questions and meaning-making. We conceptualized these three categories in terms of *formal* interactions (those that are planned through programs) and *informal* (unplanned) interactions. Our conceptual framework is portrayed in Table 11.1.

In addition to the type (formal or informal) and nature (academic, social, or deeper life) of student-faculty interactions, we also sought to examine student awareness and perceptions of the faculty-in-residence program. We created four additional variables to measure student knowledge of the faculty-in-residence position (knowledge), perceived value of the faculty-in-residence position (value), level of comfort in approaching the faculty in residence

TABLE 11.1
Sriram and McLevain's Original Conceptual Framework of Student-Faculty Interaction

	Academic	Social	Deeper Life
Informal engagement (nonprogrammatic)	Informal academic	Informal social	Informal deeper life
Formal engagement (programmatic)	Formal academic	Formal social	Formal deeper life

(comfort), and perception of the faculty's contribution to the norms of the environment (experience).

In case you lost count, that adds up to 10 latent variables. How could we know if these were true latent variables or not? Is comfort, for example, really a latent variable separate from experience? Exploratory factor analysis to the rescue! We took our 73-item instrument and administered it to two residential colleges at two distinct institutions, both of which are research institutions in different regions of the United States. We conducted a principal components analysis, and we used eigenvalues, scree plots, and total variance explained to determine how many latent variables to retain from our data. We ultimately decided to move forward with only five latent variables (factors). The principal components analysis suggested there was not a meaningful difference between formal and informal interactions as we had originally hypothesized. In other words, we were wrong in thinking that planned and unplanned interactions had different influences on students. Furthermore, the analysis failed to isolate comfort and experience as distinct variables, despite our original theory. The elimination of the comfort and experience latent variables, along with the integration of the formal and informal qualifiers, left us with five valid latent variables: knowledge, value, social interaction, academic interaction, and deeper life interaction.

In a follow-up study, we administered our survey once again and conducted a confirmatory factor analysis. We wanted to validate a model of how these variables interact, that is, how student-faculty interaction with faculty in residence works. Although it was not as simple and easy as I am making it sound, we eventually validated a model shown in Figure 11.4.

Figure 11.4. Structural equation model for student-faculty interaction.

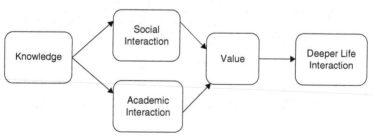

We found that knowledge of the faculty in residence leads to social and academic interactions between the faculty in residence and students. These interactions lead students to place more value on the faculty-in-residence role. This increased value thereby leads to increased deeper life interactions (conversations about life's big questions and meaning-making) between the faculty in residence and students. The result was a theory (way of explaining things) about student-faculty interaction that was based on data. Table 11.2 provides a summary of factor analysis.

TABLE 11.2
Factory Analysis Summary Table

	Exploratory Factor Analysis (Principal Components Analysis)	**Confirmatory Factor Analysis (Structural Equation Modeling)**
Type of question	Analyzing structure: Validating latent variables	Analyzing structure: Confirming a model
Interpreting results	Eigenvalues, scree plots, and total variance explained	Confirmatory fit index and root mean square error of approximation
The gift (what you get)	An objective, statistics-based assessment of what latent variables exist in your data (how your item responses group together)	A validated theory (way of explaining things) or model based on the patterns found in your data
Sample size guide	Ideal is 300, but it is possible to get good results with less	Ideal is 300, but it is possible to get good results with less

Review Questions From This Chapter

Use the following review questions to test yourself. When you test yourself, you force yourself to recall information, and the act of recalling leads to better and deeper learning.

- What type of question does factor analysis answer?
- What are the two types of factor analysis, and what is the difference between them?
- What do you get from the two types of factor analysis?

Homework

My example in this chapter discusses confirmatory factor analysis (structural equation modeling). For an example of exploratory factor analysis (principal components analysis), please search the Internet for the following article, and read it:

> Sriram, R. (2014a). Development, validity, and reliability of a psychometric instrument measuring competencies in student affairs. *Journal of Student Affairs Research and Practice, 51*(4), 349–363.

In this article I discuss creating an instrument to measure competencies in student affairs professionals. It is an example of how factor analysis can be a way to do student affairs slow for the betterment of student affairs professionals (and therefore the betterment college students as well).

12

HOW THIS BOOK SHOULD CHANGE YOUR LIFE

You are in a unique class of professionals. I know this because you are not only the type of person to buy this book but also the type of person to read it. You are a scholar practitioner. The world needs you. Our colleges and universities need you. Most important, our students need you. I am guessing I can divide the information you have read in this book into three learning categories: deep learning, surface learning, and not learned yet. The first category, deep learning, is the information you learned that has stuck with you. You have either already applied it or thought about how you can apply it soon. The amount of information in this category is likely pretty small. The second category, surface learning, pertains to the information that made sense to you at the time but has faded away since. For example, perhaps the difference between parametric and nonparametric statistics made complete sense to you earlier, but you could not explain these concepts now or map them onto your statistics scaffold. The third category, not learned yet, represents the information you were not quite ready to learn (your brain was too full) or that you did not want to learn (you did not care). I am estimating that 20% of the information in this book is deep learning for you, 60% is surface learning, and 20% is not learned yet.

That's not good enough. Yes, it's a start, but how do we get you where you need to be? That is what this chapter is about. I want this book to change your life so that you can change the lives of college students for the better. Changing your life means changing your behaviors. Changing your behaviors means altering the way you do things today and tomorrow. It requires student affairs fast and student affairs slow. There is no time for someday. The cost is too high. Our students need you now.

Overview

I was once a student affairs professional who did not know anything about statistics. I learned statistics because I began to realize its power in helping to change the world for the better. It takes time to learn these skills. There is no such thing as a math brain, and you must keep a growth mind-set along the way. This chapter contains my advice on how to continue your journey as a developing scholar practitioner. My advice highlights what has worked for me and what has worked for others (based on feedback I received on presentations and publications).

Before I delve into that advice, I need to ask you a big favor: Please read this book again. I cannot fully express how much reading books on statistics multiple times helped me to deeply learn the content. This book is long enough that you most likely forgot what was discussed in the first chapters. Those chapters, I believe, will mean even more to you now. From research design to scale development to basic statistics to inferential statistics, too much is covered in the later chapters of this book for you to deeply learn in one reading. By reading those chapters again, you will build on the foundation laid during your first reading. You will not regret reading this book again.

Research Behaviors (Individual and Communal)

The following are 10 things I want you to do to change your life. The first 6 have to do with you as an individual and your research behaviors. The last 4 (7 through 10) have to do with your entire division of student affairs and developing a research culture.

1. Learn descriptive statistics and effect size.
2. Practice the First 15 (explained later).
3. Become an expert (read research topically).
4. Share your expertise.
5. Use good books as guides.
6. Pick a project and pursue it.
7. Begin a reading or research group.
8. Commit to discoveries for the long term.
9. Demand it in writing.
10. Hold each other accountable.

Learn Descriptive Statistics and Effect Size

The four types of descriptive statistics are helpful and powerful. Learn them by heart and force yourself to use them in practice. After a few times of forcing yourself, you will become addicted. At that point, no one can stop you. For review, the four types of descriptive statistics (with the most common calculation in parentheses) are central tendency (average), variance (standard deviation), relative position (z-scores or percentile ranks), and relationship (correlation).

You already know how to use average. By adding standard deviation (a measure of variance) to your current knowledge of average, you will greatly increase your statistical sophistication in one easy step. Standard deviation is the average distance of scores from the average. The closer the standard deviation is to zero, the better the average is at representing a group of scores. Relative position, or z-scores, translates the scores in your group to a new score that represents standard deviation. So a z-score of 1 means that a particular score is one standard deviation above the average. The z-scores are helpful because you can immediately see how a particular score relates to the group as a whole (without having to look at any reference point). Correlations are the baseline of all statistics. Correlations (i.e., regressions) display the corelationship between two variables on a scale from −1.0 to +1.0. And remember: All these calculations can be performed using Microsoft Excel.

Effect size matters much more than statistical significance. Effect size represents how big an influence, impact, or effect one variable has on another. Statistical significance is whether the effect seen in your sample can also be inferred in your population. There are two primary ways to determine effect size. One is to square the correlation (r^2). By squaring the correlation, you get a percentage of how much one variable accounts for another variable. This effect size is used when examining the relationship among variables. The other common way to explain effect size is in standard deviation units (e.g., Cohen's *d*). This effect size is used when comparing groups. When an effect is 0.15 standard deviation, it is small but meaningful. A medium effect is 0.3 standard deviation, and a large effect is 0.5 standard deviation (Mayhew et al., 2016).

Please learn the four types of descriptive statistics and effect size by heart. It will change your life. If that in itself feels like a big step, then I will give you a smaller one. If after reading this book you are never given an average by someone else without asking for the standard deviation, and you are never told that something is statistically significant without asking for the effect size, I will consider your time spent reading this book well worth it.

Practice the First 15

In Chapter 1, I referenced Charles Duhigg's (2012) groundbreaking and bestselling book *The Power of Habit: Why We Do What We Do in Life and Business*. In his book, Duhigg, who is a journalist, summarizes the research of others on what habits are and how to develop them. Habits are when the brain takes a sequence of actions and chunks them into an automatic routine, thereby saving effort and improving efficiency. Habits make up about 40% of our daily decisions.

The power of habit, Duhigg (2012) explains, is when you understand the habit process and purposefully manipulate it. Habits have three parts: a cue, a behavior, and a reward. The cue is something that triggers the habit, whether it is the time of day, a certain place, or even a particular emotion. This cue alerts the brain that it is time to enact a habit. This happens so quickly and easily that you do not notice it. But identifying and focusing your attention on the cue can help you to form or change a habit. The second step in the process is the habit itself. The third step is the reward. This may seem odd, but a habit rewards you in some way. Duhigg refers to it as fulfilling a craving. When you enact a habit, there is a feeling of satisfaction or control.

Why am I spending time explaining habits in a book about statistics? Because changing the way you do your work will involve changing your current habits and developing new ones. And there is one habit in particular that I want you to develop. I want you to practice the First 15.

Nobody has time to read. You have to create that time within your current constraints. But, as Steven Sample (2003), a former president of the University of Southern California, once wrote, "You are what you read" (p. 55). Reading is an absolute, nonnegotiable component to your development as a scholar practitioner. So how do you create the time to read? You create it by developing the habit of the First 15.

I want you to spend the first 15 minutes of every workday reading. When you walk into your office in the morning, I want you to put your stuff down, avoid your computer, sit in your chair, grab a book or article, set a timer for 15 minutes, and start reading. Every day. Do not ever let anything get in the way of your 15 minutes unless it is an emergency. On the other hand, do not ever let yourself go over the 15 minutes. The reason is that if you start letting yourself go over 15 minutes, you will quit the habit altogether because it requires too much time from your day.

There is something magical about 15 minutes. It is enough time to really accomplish something. Yet it is also a small enough chunk of time to do something consistently and defend it vigorously. Charles Eliot ("Eliot Names Books," 1909), a famous president of Harvard who edited *The Harvard Classics,* once said that anyone could have the equivalent of a Harvard education by reading from his selected list of books for 15 minutes a day. Steven Sample carved out 20 minutes a day to read even while serving as president of a major research university.

I recommend 15 minutes of reading a day, but it must be the first 15 minutes. The day will get too busy otherwise. People will find you, and they will demand you. But during those first minutes in your office, people tend to leave you alone. People are still waking up, and the caffeine from their coffee has not kicked in yet. Walking into your office is the cue. Reading for 15 minutes is the automatic routine. And the feeling of investing in your own development as a scholar practitioner is the reward. You will soon be amazed at how much you read over time with such a short daily commitment.

Become an Expert (Read Research Topically)

If you are reading for 15 minutes every day, a natural question that follows is, What should you read? This is important. You should not use this time to catch up on the latest novel. This time should be reserved for developing yourself as an expert. Experts have expertise because they devote time to knowing something with a level of depth that goes beyond what others have. You must decide what you want to develop your expertise in and start finding good things to read on that topic.

A common mistake student affairs professionals make is thinking that they need to read everything research-wise that is thrown at them. Each month, you get e-mails from journals listing the latest research on a wide variety of subtopics in higher education. Reading all those articles will exhaust you, bore you, and not really develop your expertise. Reading what others send you is a passive approach. I want you to take a proactive approach.

Being proactive begins with choosing a subtopic. If you are a residence life professional, perhaps you want to become an expert on the research directly involving residence life. Or perhaps you are interested in a more specialized subtopic such as living-learning programs. If you work with fraternities and sororities, perhaps you want to become an expert on what the research has to say about these student organizations. The choice is yours.

When you have your subtopic, you need to find interesting things to read on it. Google Scholar is a great resource for journal articles. There may also be books related to what you want to know. Please—I beg you—start with the articles or books that appear to be the most interesting to you. Base your decision on titles and abstracts. Once you have picked your article or book, acquire it through the library and spend your 15 minutes a day reading it. When you are done, pick another on the same subtopic. Repeat this cycle until you have read everything on your subtopic or until you feel ready to move on to another subtopic. Soon you will find you are an expert on the topic.

Share Your Expertise

There is little point to developing your expertise if you do not share it with others. Sharing your expertise is easier said than done, however. On a college campus, plenty of people need your expertise, and plenty do not want your expertise. You likely have not thought of the act of sharing your expertise as a learnable skill, but it is. It takes practice and confidence. The confidence comes from the time you spend developing your expertise (practicing the First 15) and the time you spend practicing how to share your expertise.

Student affairs professionals bring something important to the proverbial table. Often their expertise gets pushed aside. If you have experienced this, I am sorry. At the same time, I need to tell you that you are partly responsible. You must be proactive, professional, and persistent in sharing your expertise with others.

One of my favorite concepts to teach my students is sense-making, which is working with others to create a shared interpretation of reality (Birnbaum, 1988; Weick, Sutcliffe, & Obstfeld, 2005). When you understand sense-making, you stop trying to change other people's behaviors and instead try to shift their perception of reality. Once their view of reality changes, their behaviors will follow.

Student affairs professionals must look for opportunities to share their knowledge, which will shape other people's view of reality. Shaping their reality will shape their behaviors. You must share. This does not mean you should wait until asked. If you are in the room, you have already been asked to some degree. When they hired you, they asked. When you were put on the committee, they asked. When you were invited to the meeting, they asked. No one is going to pause the conversation, turn to you, and say, Do you have anything helpful to add to this conversation? Everyone will instead assume that if you had something helpful to say, you would offer it. So offer it.

This is where published research can be extremely helpful to your work as it carries with it an incredible amount of credibility on the college campus. It also takes the pressure off you and helps you to come across as humble in your remarks. After all, you are simply sharing the knowledge of other scholars, not plugging your own work.

You should practice a one- to two-minute elevator speech explaining why your work matters based on research. If you carry this with you and refine it as you go, you will be surprised how useful it becomes. People from around campus will say stupid things about your work, and you must respond to stupid statements with intelligent answers, not defensiveness. The following are some examples of what colleagues around campus might say about your work along with some suggested responses.

> Colleague: I've seen the work you do during orientation. It's really just fun and games. The work I do is serious.
>
> Response: I agree that the work you do is serious and important. I know that some of our work can look like merely fun and games, but the research is pretty clear that sense of belonging is a key to success for students. When students feel they belong, they are able to put more effort into their studies, and they are significantly more likely to stay at the institution. I don't care about fun and games, but I do care about students and their sense of belonging. If fun and games can help increase that sense of belonging, especially at a critical transition time like orientation, then I consider such work a privilege to do. If you want to see an example of this research on the importance of sense of belonging, I would be happy to e-mail you an article.

> Colleague: We waste a lot of money on these activities for kids.
>
> Response: With all due respect, they are not kids. They are adults with adult responsibilities and adult problems. And what evidence do you have that we are wasting any money? The evidence I see in research is that the work we do with students out of class not only improves their academic experiences but also plays a key role in retaining them at our institution. This is an investment with a big return by keeping students here and giving them an experience they will appreciate as alumni.

> Colleague: It's crazy how much money we spend on dorms just to make students excited. Let them live in apartments off campus so that we can spend our money elsewhere.
>
> Response: Dorm comes from the Latin *dormire* which means to sleep. Dorms were once places where students would sleep and do nothing else, especially after World War II. We are now establishing residential communities where learning is embraced and

encouraged. If a student is in class 15 hours a week, that student is not in class almost 100 waking hours every week. If we are not using those 100 hours to amplify the 15 hours in class, then we are wasting a great opportunity and wasting students' money. We want residential communities to be places where students can study, engage with faculty informally, and even possibly attend class. The research clearly demonstrates that living on campus significantly and positively affects retention and grades. Using campus living to fulfill the mission of the university is one of the surest investments we can make based on research.

You have your own style for responding. But can you see how these examples can potentially shift people's interpretation of the present situation? Hurt feelings and defensiveness will not do that. So do not merely develop your expertise and keep it to yourself. The real power will come from the sense-making you do based on your expertise.

Use Good Books as Guides

I have read a lot of books on statistics. They are not all created equal. My frustration with what is currently offered led me to write this book. But there are other fantastic books out there that I want to recommend to you and that are organized under the following categories: motivational, statistics, survey development, and reference.

Motivational. This one might seem like an odd category, but there are books that have more to do with the motivation behind using quantitative research and statistics then they do with statistical techniques. My favorite book in this category is by Ian Ayres (2008) called *Super Crunchers: Why Thinking-by-Numbers Is the New Way to Be Smart.* Ayres does a fabulous job discussing the relationship between intuition (thinking fast) and logic (thinking slow). His examples are interesting, and his arguments are compelling. I think *Super Crunchers* will help you think outside the box on how you can use quantitative research and statistics in your work in student affairs. I also recommend Lisa Hatfield and Vicki Wise's (2015) *A Guide to Becoming a Scholarly Practitioner in Student Affairs.* Hatfield and Wise discuss why scholarship is important in our field and provide tips for writing and presenting.

Statistics. Although my book is meant to be a gateway into other statistics books, there are a couple of statistics books I really like.

The first one is Andy Field's (2013) *Discovering Statistics Using IBM SPSS Statistics.* Field is a gifted teacher, and he understands how helpful humor can be when trying to teach statistics. His book has a lot of information, but it all builds on the foundation I already laid in this book. I also like Field's book because he explains how to conduct all the statistical techniques using IBM SPSS, which I think is the statistical software with the best balance between usability and functionality.

A close second to Field's book is Mertler and Reinhart's (2017) *Advanced and Multivariate Statistical Methods.* It is clearly written, organized well, and provides step-by-step instructions on how to conduct each statistical technique.

Survey development. I was at a conference when one of the presenters mentioned a great book on how to properly develop surveys. I wrote down the author's name and title and eventually ordered a copy. I do not know where I would be as a scholar if I had not read that book. *Scale Development: Theory and Applications,* by Robert DeVellis (2017), is the go-to text on how to develop a psychometric instrument. Most of what I teach you about scales comes from that book. If developing scales fascinates you, then please read DeVellis's book.

I also want to recommend a few articles by Stephen Porter, a professor who is interested in higher education and quantitative research methods. Porter's (2011) article "Do College Student Surveys Have Any Validity?" is a must-read for anyone conducting surveys on college campuses. Another article from Porter (2003), "The Impact of Lottery Incentives on Student Survey Response Rates," discusses the research behind ways to improve response rates (which continue to drop in college student research).

Reference. Wouldn't it be nice if someone took all the statistical terminology and jargon and made a dictionary just for statistics? Vogt and Johnson (2011) did just that in their *Dictionary of Statistics & Methodology,* and the book is an absolute treasure. What I find especially weird is how often I look up terms I already know just to be sure I have them right in my head. The book is so easy to use, and I am glad they spent countless hours creating this book for my benefit. This book will increase your learning by making it simple to look up statistical facts.

Pick a Project and Pursue It

I am not a perfectionist, and I consider that a gift. If you are a perfectionist, you will need to find a way to reign in your expectations. To learn statistics, you must do statistics. To do statistics, you must pick a project and pursue it. You might be scared at first about making mistakes. Trust me, you will make mistakes. The only way not to make mistakes is to make mistakes, learn from them, and then stop making them. Yes, there is a lot to be said about planning and preparation (not to mention the time you spend reading books like this one). But there are many details that only experience teaches you how to handle. So pick a project and pursue it.

On the one hand, you should pick something you are truly interested in for the long term. On the other hand, you are not signing your life away by picking a project. The advantage to picking a project you are invested in for the long term is that the mistakes you make along the way can be quickly corrected in the next iteration. In other words, if you can pick a research quest that you can do every semester, you will continue to improve it each and every semester. If you cannot do it every semester, then do it every year and make refinements. In five years, you will have not only lots of data but also a fine-tuned process on how to conduct research. Mastering one project sets you up for success in your next project. So pick a topic, choose a research design, develop a scale, think about possible statistical approaches, and begin.

Begin a Reading or Research Group

These last four suggestions pertain to creating a research culture. Culture drives behavior (Schein, 2010). I dream of a day when divisions of student affairs become cultures that foster scholar practitioners. My suggestion is to form a reading group or a research group. A reading group chooses a book (like this one) and goes through it with a small group of dedicated professionals. A research group comes together regularly to discuss research ideas, progress, struggles, and findings. Taking a journey in community is more fun, and it is transformational. I have been a part of such groups in the past, and I loved the experience. In fact, I ended up joining such a group while writing this book.

With the immense help of two graduate students, I put together a scholar practitioner workshop for the division of student affairs on our campus. During the latter part of the fall semester, we advertised the workshop, distributed flyers, and even put together a video advertisement. A dean in the division of student affairs agreed to pay for refreshments for the meetings as well as supplies such as binders and notebooks. We told potential participants that the workshop would take place over 12 weeks in the spring semester, and if they missed more than two sessions, they would be asked to leave the group. We were serious about this.

To our delight, 10 student affairs professionals signed up for the workshop, making us a group of 13 when you include the two graduate students and myself. The workshop was essentially a blended class and reading group. We blocked off 10:00 a.m. to 11:45 a.m. on participants' calendars and met almost every week, three times a month. We spent the time as follows:

- 10:00 a.m.–10:30 a.m.: Time set aside to read the chapter in one's own office
- 10:30 a.m.–10:45 a.m.: Time set aside for walking to the meeting location
- 10:45 a.m.–11:45 a.m.: Time for discussion

Even though we blocked off almost two hours of time for participants, we only met for discussion for one hour. Thirty minutes was built in for reading so that participants were without the excuse that they could not read the designated chapter. At worst, they could at least skim the material beforehand.

The meetings were centered on the chapters of this book (which were in draft form at the time). We read one to two chapters per session. The times together were almost always full of open discussion, so we used the following four prompts to guide our meetings:

1. Light bulb for, What insights did you gain from this passage?
2. Question mark for, What confused you? What questions do you have?
3. Ear for, Do you know someone who needs to hear this passage? Who? Why?

4. Arrow for, What will you do differently as a result of reading
   this passage?

I asked participants to keep these four prompts in mind as they read.
Then, we would go through the prompts one by one as a means
of drawing out discussion. I would ask, What light bulbs did we
have? After a few seconds of silence, someone would share a light
bulb thought. That first comment would bring out other light bulb
moments in the room, and soon we would have a wonderful discussion.
When it began to die down, I would then ask, Who has question
marks? Using this format, we would fly through the hour with
very little awkwardness.

Two hours almost every week is a lot to ask from busy student
affairs professionals. Therefore, I asked each person to say why he or
she decided to attend the workshop. The comments were inspiring
in their feelings of hope and honesty. For many, it felt as if they were
finally invited to talk about the metaphorical elephant they felt in
the room of their careers. One participant was grateful that someone
was finally calling her out on not being a scholar practitioner, and
she was ready to do something about it. Another talked about the
need for student affairs professionals to make their expertise known,
especially as college administrators look for places to cut budgets.
One of my favorite comments from that first meeting was when a
participant bluntly stated: "We always talk about best practices. Best
practices are simply what other campuses are doing because those
campuses have seen other campuses doing it. Best practices are really
a very low bar to try to reach."

Commit to Discoveries for the Long Term

I mentioned the importance of long-term projects earlier. This concept
is even more important for a division of student affairs. You are
not going to get instant results from research projects. To discover
truth on your campus, you need time. If you plan to develop your
own survey scales, you need time to form and test those scales. Some
of the initial research you do with students may be more about refining
your instrument than getting results.

Also, one of the biggest hurdles to conducting quantitative
research is the need to acquire large sample sizes. If collecting a large

enough sample size in one attempt seems unrealistic, then you can take another approach. Conduct the research over several semesters with different students (who still represent your population of interest) and combine the data to achieve a larger sample size over time. This approach also requires a commitment to long-term discovery.

Understanding the work required to conduct quantitative research and statistics should lead to a sense of urgency about the need for high-level discussions among campus leaders regarding what they want to know. You do not want to be a year into a project only to have a supervisor tell you she wants to go in a different direction. Create a multiyear plan that campus leaders understand and support.

Demand It in Writing

The purpose of this book is not for you to publish in peer-reviewed journals. The purpose is to help you become a scholar practitioner who uses quantitative research to discover truth. I like peer-reviewed journals, but research at the local level is the most important research because it allows you to change the lives of the students you work with on your campus. This kind of research is difficult to publish because journals want research that is representative and generalizable.

This does not get you off the hook, however, from putting your findings in writing. You must preserve your work through writing. Writing develops your expertise and helps you to create a shared interpretation of the nature of reality (sense-making). Writing captures the vast amount of work that was done and allows it to live on forever.

You never know when a research project you conducted in the past will be helpful to you in the present. If you have to resort to oral history to convey your research, you will not only come across as less impressive but also forget much of the work you did. I am constantly amazed at my ability to forget my own work. I never thought I would read my own research, but I do so just to remind myself of the details of what was done and what was found.

When you write down your research, I suggest you follow the traditional structure: introduction, literature review, methods, results, and discussion, all sections you find in many journal articles. They do not, however, need to be as long as sections in journal articles. Short is helpful to the writer and the reader. Introduce the topic and the problem and why anyone should care about it. For the literature review, demonstrate that your search for truth is based on other people's search for truth. What did they do, what did they find, and how does it fit within the context of your research? For the methods, describe in a fair amount of detail what you did to conduct your research. This should include research design and statistical approaches. The results section should present the facts of your findings with no judgment or interpretation. Your discussion, by contrast, should discuss your results based on how it fits with the previous literature and your own interpretation (keeping in mind conclusion validity). The discussion should convey what your research means for current practice and future research.

Your writing should be sent to all interested campus leaders. It should be kept in a place where others can access it after you leave the position. When you discuss your research project in your work, you should offer to send your paper on it to any interested parties who are not familiar with it. If you are supervising someone conducting research, you should make it clear that a written report is expected. Written reports are gifts that keep on giving.

Hold Each Other Accountable

The search for truth is exciting and important. Accountability should not be the primary reason for conducting research. People tend to do what they are held accountable for doing, however. This will certainly be true for quantitative research because of the great amount of knowledge and hard work it requires. Student affairs professionals must hold one another accountable for thinking slow.

As a supervisor, conducting quantitative research and working with statistics should be an expectation of the job. This includes encouragement for your professionals to devote the time to learn quantitative research and statistics. Encourage your staff to practice the First 15 and to maintain a growth mind-set about skills they do not yet possess. Encourage them to use professional development funds to learn skills instead of only passively attending conferences. Use performance appraisals as opportunities to discuss what evidence has been gathered to support the work your professionals do. What are they learning? What are they failing in, and what evidence do they have to support their conclusions? If you can foster a culture that appreciates truth more than pretending to have good results, then people will be honest about what is not working and will have the courage (and support) to change it.

If you are not a supervisor, you still have a big role to play in holding people accountable. The first person to hold accountable for being a scholar practitioner is yourself. Model good habits and develop your expertise. When potential decisions are debated by members on your team, ask what evidence has been gathered to help with those decisions. Offer yourself as someone who is willing to help gather such evidence if it does not exist. Avoid sounding arrogant or judgmental, but you still need to ask these questions. Even if team members shrug their shoulders in response, you have sent a message that something important is missing.

Conclusion

In the Introduction, I discussed the notion of the research competency and how it can be subdivided into research values, research skills, research behaviors, and research culture (see Figure 12.1).

This summarizes my goals for you with this book. I want you to value research in student affairs practice. I want you to know how to conduct research, and I want research to be part of your everyday practice. I also want your increased research competence to positively influence your division of student affairs and your campus. The scope of this book is quantitative research and statistics, but qualitative research is also important and worthy of your time and attention.

I know your intuition and experience in student affairs (student affairs fast) matters. But I also know that the kind of college experience students deserve requires logic, reason, and the use of research (student affairs slow). Our colleges and college students need student affairs fast and slow.

You have wasted your time if you read this book without any change in your work life and habits. The changes do not have to be drastic. Small changes, done consistently, are often the most powerful forms of transformation. And transformation is what I am after.

Figure 12.1. The research competency in student affairs.

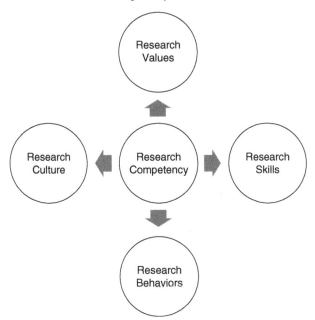

I want to transform how student affairs professionals do their work. I want to transform how student affairs professionals make decisions. I want to transform the experience of college students for the better. The list of things I want for you that I have provided in this chapter is a great place to start. Pick one or two items on this list and focus your attention there. Do not look for or expect others around you to applaud your progress along the way. They probably will not notice. But that is okay, because becoming a scholar practitioner is not about you. It is about the students you have the privilege of serving, leading, and educating every day.

APPENDIX

Final Exam

A t the end of most chapters in this book, I provide review
questions. Well, here is your final exam. Use the following
review questions to test yourself. When you test yourself,
you force yourself to recall information, and the act of recalling leads
to better and deeper learning. There is always more to learn, but if
you can answer these questions, I think you are in great shape as
a scholar practitioner. If a question stumps you, go back to that
chapter and read the corresponding section. If you turn to these
questions and quiz yourself every so often, you will master these
concepts. Then you can put them to use for the benefit of college
students.

Chapter 1

What does it mean to think fast?
What does it mean to think slow?
How can you learn to think slow more often in your work in
student affairs?

Chapter 2

What is research?
What is epistemology?
Can you list and describe the two most common epistemologies?
What is a theory?
Why are theories useful?
What is the scientific method?
What epistemology does the scientific method come from?

Chapter 3

What does it mean to have a research paradigm?
How can a research paradigm lead to more challenging and more meaningful work?
What is a growth mind-set, and why is it important?
What can research on talent and expertise mean for you as you try to learn quantitative research methods and statistics?
What is the difference between assessment and research? (Careful: This is a trick question.)

Chapter 4

What are the two and a half research designs you should know?
Which research design is better and why?
What are the four types of research questions for quantitative research?

Chapter 5

What is measurement?
What is a latent variable?
What is a true score?
What is a scale?
What is validity?
What are the Four Cs of validity?
What is reliability?

Chapter 6

What does it mean for an item to be double barreled?
What is one way to improve the validity of your scale?
What is the minimum number of respondents you need to test your scale? What is an ideal number of respondents?
What is the recommended method for checking reliability called?
What is the minimum score for a scale to be considered reliable?
What are the advantages and disadvantages to having more items in a scale?

Chapter 7

What is the difference between the two types of statistics: descriptive and inferential?

What are the four types of descriptive statistics?

What is one primary way of calculating each of the four types of descriptive statistics?

What is the normal distribution?

What is the difference between parametric and nonparametric statistics?

What does the central limit theorem state, and how is it helpful?

What does the 68-95-99 rule state, and how is it helpful?

What is statistical significance?

What is effect size, and how does it differ from statistical significance?

What are the two primary ways of calculating effect size?

How does the size of your sample affect your results?

What are the three categories of variables, and how do they differ?

Chapter 8

What type of question does multiple regression answer?

What do you get from a multiple regression?

What do you know about independent and dependent variables in a multiple regression?

How do you judge effect size in a multiple regression?

Chapter 9

What type of question does ANOVA answer?

What are the different types of ANOVA, and what do they accomplish? (e.g., MANOVA)

What do you know about independent and dependent variables in an ANOVA?

How do you judge effect size in an ANOVA?

Chapter 10

What type of question does logistic regression answer?

What do you know about independent and dependent variables in a logistic regression?

How do you judge effect size in a logistic regression?

Chapter 11

What type of question does factor analysis answer?
What are the two types of factor analysis, and what is the difference between them?
What do you get from the two types of factor analysis?

REFERENCES

Allen, K. (2002). The purpose of scholarship, redefining meaning in student affairs. *NASPA Journal, 39*, 147–157.

American College Personnel Association & NASPA–Student Affairs Professionals in Higher Education. (2010). *Professional competency areas for student affairs practitioners.* Washington, DC: Author.

American Council on Education. (1949). *The student personnel point of view.* Washington, DC: Author.

American Psychological Association. (2010). *Publication manual of the American Psychological Association.* Washington, DC: Author.

Astin, A. W. (1984). Student involvement: A developmental theory for higher education. *Journal of College Student Development, 40*, 518–529.

Ayres, I. (2007). *Super crunchers: Why thinking-by-numbers is the new way to be smart.* New York, NY: Bantam.

Bentley-Edwards, K. L., Agonafer, E., Edmondson, R., & Flannigan, A. (2016). If I can do for my people, I can do for myself: Examining racial factors for their influence on goal efficacy for Black college students. *Journal of College Student Development, 57*, 151–167.

Berger, P. L., & Luekmann, T. (1967). *The social construction of reality: A treatise in the sociology of knowledge.* Garden City, NJ: Anchor.

Bingham, M. A., & Solverson, N. W. (2016). Using enrollment data to predict retention rate. *Journal of Student Affairs Research and Practice, 53*, 51–64.

Birnbaum, R. (1988). *How colleges work.* San Francisco, CA: Jossey-Bass.

Blackwell, L. S., Trzesniewski, K. H., & Dweck, C. S. (2007). Implicit theories of intelligence predict achievement across an adolescent transition: A longitudinal study and an intervention. *Child Development, 78*, 246–263.

Blimling, G. S. (2011). How are dichotomies such as scholar/practitioner and theory/practice helpful and harmful to the profession? In P. M. Magolda & M. B. Baxter Magolda (Eds.), *Contested issues in student affairs* (pp. 42–53). Sterling, VA: Stylus.

Braxton, J. M., Doyle, W. R., Hartley, H. V., Hirschy, A. S., Jones, W. A., & McLendon, M. (2014). *Rethinking college student retention.* San Francisco, CA: Jossey-Bass.

Broido, E. M. (2011). Moving beyond dichotomies: Integrating theory, scholarship, experience, and practice. In P. M. Magolda & M. B. Baxter Magolda (Eds.), *Contested issues in student affairs* (pp. 54–59). Sterling, VA: Stylus.

Brown, P. C., Roediger, H. L., & McDaniel, M. A. (2014). *Make it stick: The science of successful learning.* Cambridge, MA: Belknap Press.

Byrne, B. M. (2010). *Structural equation modeling with AMOS.* New York, NY: Routledge.

Castellanos, J., Gloria, A. M., Mayorga, M., & Salas, C. (2007). Student affairs professionals' self-report of multicultural competence: Understanding awareness, knowledge, and skills. *NASPA Journal, 44,* 643–663.

Cho, A. R., & Sriram, R. (2016). Student affairs collaborating with academic affairs: Perceptions of individual competency and institutional culture. *College Student Affairs Journal, 34*(1), 56–69.

Cohen, J. (1988). *Statistical power analysis for the behavioral sciences.* Hillsdale, NJ: Erlbaum.

Cohen, J. (1992). A power primer. *Psychological Bulletin, 112,* 155–159.

Covey, S. R. (2004). *The 7 habits of highly effective people.* New York, NY: Free Press.

Creswell, J. W. (2014). *Research design* (4th ed.). Thousand Oaks, CA: Sage.

Crotty, M. (2003). *The foundations of social research.* Thousand Oaks, CA: Sage.

Cruce, T. M. (2009). A note on the calculation and interpretation of the delta-p statistic for categorical independent variables. *Research in Higher Education, 50,* 608–622.

DeVellis, R. F. (2017). *Scale development: Theory and applications* (4th ed.). Los Angeles, CA: Sage.

Duhigg, C. (2012). *The power of habit.* New York, NY: Random House.

Dweck, C. (2006). *Mindset: The new psychology of success.* New York, NY: Random House.

Eliot names books for 5-foot library. (1909, June 17). *New York Times,* 1. Retrieved from http://query.nytimes.com/gst/abstract.html?res=F6081 1F93C5512738DDDAE0994DE405B898CF1D3

Ericsson, K. A., Krampe, R. T., & Tesch-Romer, C. (1993). The role of deliberate practice in expert performance. *Psychological Review, 100,* 363–406.

Ericsson, K. A., & Pool, R. (2016). *Peak: Secrets from the new science of expertise.* Boston, MA: Houghton Mifflin Harcourt.

Evans, N. J., & Guido, F. M. (2012). Response to Patrick Love's "Informal Theory": A rejoinder. *Journal of College Student Development, 53,* 192–200.

Evans, N. J., & Reason, R. D. (2001). Guiding principles: A review and analysis of student affairs philosophical statements. *Journal of College Student Development, 42,* 359–377.

Field, A. (2013). *Discovering statistics using IBM SPSS Statistics* (4th ed.). Thousand Oaks, CA: Sage.

Fields, D. (2008). White matter matters. *Scientific American, 298*(3), 54–61.

Fried, J. (2002). The scholarship of student affairs: Integration and application. *NASPA Journal, 39,* 120–131.

Gladwell, M. (2005). *Blink: The power of thinking without thinking.* New York, NY: Little, Brown.

Godin, S. (2016, January 3). Software is testing [Web log post]. Retrieved from http://sethgodin.typepad.com/seths_blog/2016/01/software-is-testing.html

Hacker, A., & Dreifus, C. (2010). *Higher education? How colleges are wasting our money and failing our kids—and what we can do about it.* New York, NY: Times Books.

Harper, W. R. (1905). *The trend in higher education.* Chicago, IL: University of Chicago Press.

Hatfield, L. J., & Wise, V. L. (2015). *A guide to becoming a scholarly practitioner in student affairs.* Sterling, VA: Stylus.

Johnson, D. R., Soldner, M., Leonard, J. B., Alvarez, P., Inkelas, K. K., Rowan-Kenyon, H. T., & Longerbeam, S. D. (2007). Examining sense of belonging among first-year undergraduates from different racial/ethnic groups. *Journal of College Student Development, 48,* 525–542.

Kahneman, D. (2011). *Thinking, fast and slow.* New York, NY: Farrar, Strauss and Giroux.

Kuh, G. D., Kinzie, J., Schuh, J. H., & Whitt, E. J. (2010). *Student success in college: Creating conditions that matter.* San Francisco, CA: Jossey-Bass.

Kuk, L., Cobb, B., & Forrest, C. S. (2007). Perceptions of competencies of entry-level practitioners in student affairs. *NASPA Journal, 44*(4), 664–691.

Levitt, S. D., & Dubner, S. J. (2006). *Freakonomics.* New York, NY: HarperCollins.

Levitt, S. D., & Dubner, S. J. (2014). *Think like a freak.* New York, NY: HarperCollins.

Lincoln, Y. S., & Guba, E. G. (1985). *Naturalistic inquiry.* Beverly Hills, CA: Sage.

Love, P. (2012). Informal theory: The ignored link in theory-to-practice. *Journal of College Student Development, 53,* 177–199.

Malaney, G. D. (2002). Scholarship in student affairs through teaching and research. *NASPA Journal, 39,* 132–146.

Mayhew, M. J., Rokenbach, A. N., Bowman, N. A., Seifert, T. A., Wolniak, G. C., Pascarella, E. T., & Terenzini, P. T. (2016). *How college affects students: 21st century evidence that higher education works* (Vol. 3). San Francisco, CA: Jossey-Bass.

Mertler, C. A., & Reinhart, R. V. (2017). *Advanced and multivariate statistical methods.* New York, NY: Routledge.

Nisbett, R. E. (2015). *Mindware: Tools for smart thinking.* New York, NY: Farrar, Strauss and Giroux.

Peng, C. J., & So, T. H. (2002). Logistic regression analysis and reporting: A primer. *Understanding Statistics, 1*(1), 31–70.

Porter, S. R. (2011). Do college student surveys have any validity. *Review of Higher Education, 35*(1), 45–76.

Porter, S. R., & Whitcomb, M. E. (2003). The impact of lottery incentives on student survey response rates. *Research in Higher Education, 44,* 389–407.

Renn, K. A., & Hodges, J. (2007). The first year on the job: Experiences of new professionals in student affairs. *NASPA journal, 44,* 367–391.

Sample, S. (2003). *The contrarian's guide to leadership.* San Francisco, CA: Jossey-Bass.

Schein, E. H. (2010). *Organizational culture and leadership.* San Francisco, CA: Jossey-Bass.

Schroeder, C. C., & Pike, G. R. (2001). The scholarship of application in student affairs. *Journal of College Student Development, 42,* 342–355.

Schuh, J. (2009). *Assessment methods in student affairs.* San Francisco, CA: Jossey-Bass.

Shushok, F. (2016). Complicate yourself. *About Campus, 21*(1), 2–3.

Shushok, F., & Sriram, R. (2010). Exploring the effect of a residential academic affairs–student affairs partnership: The first year of an engineering and computer science living-learning center. *Journal of College and University Student Housing, 36*(2), 68–81.

Soria, K. M., Roberts, J. E., & Reinhard, A. P. (2015). First-year college students' strengths awareness and perceived leadership development. *Journal of Student Affairs Research and Practice, 52*(1), 89–103.

Sriram, R. (2014a). Development, validity, and reliability of a psychometric instrument measuring competencies in student affairs. *Journal of Student Affairs Research and Practice, 51,* 349–363.

Sriram, R. (2014b). Rethinking intelligence: The role of mindset in promoting success for academically high-risk students. *Journal of College Student Retention: Research, Theory and Practice, 15*, 515–536.

Sriram, R. (2017). We need researchers . . . so let's stop using the term assessment. *About Campus, 22*(2), 33–36.

Sriram, R., & McLevain, M. (2016). Developing an instrument to examine student-faculty interaction in faculty-in-residence programs. *Journal of College Student Development, 57*, 604–609.

Sriram, R., & Oster, M. (2012). Reclaiming the "scholar" in scholar-practitioner. *Journal of Student Affairs Research and Practice, 49*, 377–396.

Stanovich, K. E., & West, R. F. (2000). Individual differences in reasoning: Implications for the rationality debate. *Behavioral and Brain Sciences, 23*, 645–665.

Strange, C. C., & King, P. M. (1990). The professional practice of student development. In D. G. Creamer & Associates (Eds.), *College student development: Theory and practice* (pp. 9–24). Alexandria, VA: American College Personnel Association.

Tabachnick, B. G., & Fidell, L. S. (2007). *Using multivariate statistics* (5th ed.). Boston, MA: Pearson.

Tinto, V. (1993). *Leaving college: Rethinking the causes and cures of student attrition.* Chicago, IL: University of Chicago Press.

Tourangeau, R., Rips, L. J., & Rasinski, K. (2000). *The psychology of survey response.* Cambridge, UK: Cambridge University Press.

Tull, A. (2006). Synergistic supervision, job satisfaction, and intention to turnover of new professionals in student affairs. *Journal of College Student Development, 47*, 465–477.

Vogt, W. P. & Johnson, R. B. (2011). *Dictionary of statistics & methodology* (4th. ed.). Thousand Oaks, CA: Sage.

Wadsworth, B. J. (1996). *Piaget's theory of cognitive and affective development: Foundations of constructivism.* White Plains, NY: Longman.

Waple, J. N. (2006). An assessment of skills and competencies necessary for entry-level student affairs work. *NASPA Journal, 43*, 1–18.

Weick, K. E., Sutcliffe, K. M., & Obstfeld, D. (2005). Organizing and the process of sensemaking. *Organization Science, 16*, 409–421.

Wheelan, C. (2013). *Naked statistics: Stripping the dread from the data.* New York, NY: Norton.

Young, R. B. (2001). A perspective on the values of student affairs and scholarship. *Journal of College Student Development, 42*, 319–337.

ABOUT THE AUTHOR

R ishi Sriram serves as associate professor of higher education and student affairs, associate chair for the Department of Educational Leadership, and residential college faculty steward of Brooks Residential College—a living-learning community of approximately 400 students, at Baylor University.

Sriram spent eight years as a higher education and student affairs administrator before beginning his current role as a professor. He played a primary role in the development of residential colleges and living-learning programs and in the establishment of a faculty-in-residence program at Baylor. His administrative work won him a NASPA Excellence Award (Gold Honoree) and a Promising Practices Award from the NASPA Student Affairs Partnering with Academic Affairs Knowledge Community.

Sriram's research interests include student affairs practice; collaboration between academic and student affairs; and college student retention, engagement, achievement, and learning. His work has been published in respected journals such as *Journal of College Student Development, Review of Higher Education, Journal of Student Affairs Research and Practice,* and *Journal of College Student Retention.* He has served on the editorial and review boards of several higher education journals and has also served as the first director of research for the Texas Association of College and University Student Personnel Administrators.

INDEX

Also available from Stylus

A Guide to Becoming a Scholarly Practitioner in Student Affairs

By Lisa J. Hatfield and Vicki L. Wise

Foreword by Kevin Kruger

Student affairs professionals are increasingly being called upon to become scholar practitioners, to reflect on and share their experiences to further the knowledge of the field, and to disseminate practices to promote student learning and development.

This book offers practical guidance to anyone in the field interested in presenting at conferences or publishing in scholarly and professional journals, and sets the work of scholarly practice in the context of its vital role of influencing and shaping the future of student affairs and in promoting continuous learning.

The authors demystify the processes of producing research and scholarly work; address motivation and barriers such as time constraints or confidence; and provide advice on developing ideas, writing, getting feedback, staying on task, identifying the appropriate outlets and venues for ideas, and submitting proposals, as well as on speaking and presentation skills. It also directs readers to books and online resources and presents the reflections of senior student affairs officers on scholarship in the profession.

This book is intended for student affairs professionals at all levels. It sets the context for those starting their careers as they navigate and understand their new roles; aims to inspire mid-level professionals to present or write about their experiences and contributions; and offers senior administrators strategies to pursue their own scholarship while creating a supportive environment for their staff to do so, and develop their agency and professional growth in the process.

"This is a practical guide that will inspire student affair educators to become scholar practitioners. By demystifying the presentation and publication process, the authors provide step-by-step insights and guidance for promoting the worthwhile scholarship of student affairs professionals."—**Sarah Marshall**, *Associate Professor of Educational Leadership and Director of the Doctor of Education Program at Central Michigan University*

22883 Quicksilver Drive
Sterling, VA 20166-2102   Subscribe to our e-mail alerts: www.Styluspub.com